Time for German

All it takes is twenty minutes a day

Corinna Schicker

Stanley Thornes (Publishers) Ltd

First published in 1999 by:
Stanley Thornes (Publishers) Ltd
Ellenborough House
Wellington Street
CHELTENHAM GL50 1YW
England

99 00 01 02 03 / 10 9 8 7 6 5 4 3 2 1

A catalogue record for this book is available from the British Library

ISBN 0–7487–3878–9 (book)
ISBN 0–7487–3880–0 (complete pack)
ISBN 0–7487–3879–7 (cassettes)

Also available in the *Time for Languages* series:

Time for French, Paul Durrant
Time for Italian, Donatella de Ferra, Marina Mozzon-McPherson
Time for Portuguese, Sue Tyson-Ward
Time for Spanish, Robert Clarke

Cover: Joanna Kerr

Typeset by Action Publishing Technology Limited, Gloucester
Recorded at Matinée Sound & Vision, Reading
Voice artists: Sebastian Voss, Erich Redman, Gabriele Strutt
Printed and bound in Great Britain by T. J. International Ltd, Padstow, Cornwall

How to make the best use of *Time for German*

The material in *Time for German* has been designed for you to complete one unit every day, but you are in control. If you want to cover several units in a day, then do that. Do try, however, to stick to a sensible routine so that you cover a number of units spread over the course of one week, rather than ten sessions at the week-end. You will retain so much more if you 'drip-feed' yourself. You should ideally work through the units in sequence, but again, you are in control. Choose a method which suits you best.

Throughout the 60 units there are plenty of opportunities to practise speaking German. Start by listening to the **Vokabular** (vocabulary) section on the recording and follow the words in your book. Listen carefully to the pronunciation and try to mimic it as best you can yourself. There is space on the recording for you to repeat the word immediately after the actor. If possible, practise out loud, and don't be shy! The more you get used to hearing your own voice speaking German, the easier it will become. The vocabulary is read out on the cassette until Unit 28. In the later units you can still practise reading the words and phrases out loud; you can check your pronunciation when you listen to the dialogues.

Listen to the **Dialog** (dialogue) section, first of all without following the transcript in the book, and then using the text. See how much you can understand before you consult the text. Don't worry if there are parts you miss – just try to catch the drift of what is said.

Once you have read through the text and unravelled its contents you are ready for the **Übungen** (exercises). Listen to exercises involving the recording at least twice all the way through before you follow the prompts on the cassette or in the book to complete the exercise. You will soon get used to the method used here, and you will find it invaluable in gaining confidence in speaking naturally. Other exercises are based on text and pictures in the book, giving you the opportunity to practise the words and phrases used in the dialogues.

Finally read the **Tip** (usually a grammar hint) and **Land und Leute** which gives you some background on the culture and lifestyle of German-speaking Europe.

Do come back to units in the future to refresh your memory. Once you have covered the unit with the help of the book, you will find that playing the recordings in your car or while ironing or whatever will prove invaluable.

Good luck and enjoy learning German!

Contents

Unit 1	**Self and others**	Greetings	6
Unit 2	**Food and drink**	In the restaurant/ordering drinks	8
Unit 3	**Shopping**	Groceries	10
Unit 4	**Directions**	Asking the way	12
Unit 5	**Numbers**	Family	14
Unit 6	**Public transport**	Travelling by train	16
Unit 7	**Accommodation**	At the hotel	18
Unit 8	**Hobbies and pastimes**	Nationalities/leisure time	20
Unit 9	**Towns and villages**	Houses	22
Unit 10	**Weather**	'What's the weather like?'	24
Unit 11	**Problems**	At the chemist's	26
Unit 12	**The present, the future and the past**	Arranging to meet this week	28
Unit 13	**Self and others**	Saying where you live	30
Unit 14	**Food and drink**	In the restaurant/paying the bill	32
Unit 15	**Shopping**	Clothes	34
Unit 16	**Directions**	'I'm looking for ...'	36
Unit 17	**Numbers**	Telling the time	38
Unit 18	**Public transport**	Using public transport	40
Unit 19	**Accommodation**	Booking in advance	42
Unit 20	**Hobbies and pastimes**	Leisure time	44
Unit 21	**Towns and villages**	Sights and amenities	46
Unit 22	**Weather**	Weather forecast	48
Unit 23	**Problems**	Feeling ill/at the doctor's	50
Unit 24	**The present, the future and the past**	Arranging to meet tomorrow	52
Unit 25	**Self and others**	'May I introduce ...?'	54
Unit 26	**Food and drink**	In a café	56
Unit 27	**Shopping**	In the department store	58
Unit 28	**Directions**	By car	60
Unit 29	**Numbers**	At the cash desk	62
Unit 30	**Public transport**	Changing and getting off	64
Unit 31	**Accommodation**	At the tourist office	66
Unit 32	**Hobbies and pastimes**	Winter and summer	68
Unit 33	**Towns and villages**	Sightseeing	70
Unit 34	**Weather**	Seasons	72

| Unit 35 | **Problems** | 'I've lost something!' | 74 |
| Unit 36 | **The present, the future and the past** | Jobs | 76 |

Unit 37	**Self and others**	'What does he look like?'	78
Unit 38	**Food and drink**	Snacks	80
Unit 39	**Shopping**	Different types of food	82
Unit 40	**Directions**	'Where's the post office?'	84
Unit 41	**Numbers**	Money: Numbers over 100	86
Unit 42	**Public transport**	Travelling to work	88
Unit 43	**Accommodation**	Booking into a hotel	90
Unit 44	**Hobbies and pastimes**	'But what about the weather?'	92
Unit 45	**Towns and villages**	Sightseeing	94
Unit 46	**Weather**	More about the weather	96
Unit 47	**Problems**	Broken down	98
Unit 48	**The present, the future and the past**	Plans for tomorrow	100

Unit 49	**Self and others**	Family	102
Unit 50	**Food and drink**	Breakfast	104
Unit 51	**Shopping**	More clothes	106
Unit 52	**Directions**	'How do I get to ..?'	108
Unit 53	**Numbers**	Telephone numbers	110
Unit 54	**Public transport**	Buying a railway ticket	112
Unit 55	**Accommodation**	At the camp site	114
Unit 56	**Hobbies and pastimes**	Going on an excursion	116
Unit 57	**Towns and villages**	Staying with friends	118
Unit 58	**Weather**	More about the weather	120
Unit 59	**Problems**	Accidents and emergencies	122
Unit 60	**The present, the future and the past**	Arranging a meal	124

Answers			126
Grammar Summary			133
Vocabulary			138
Grammar and Subject Indexes			144

Self and others

Greetings

Vokabular (Basic vocabulary)

Guten Tag	good morning/good afternoon
Auf Wiedersehen	good-bye
wie heißen Sie?	what's your name?
ich heiße	my name is
ich bin	I am
Herr	Mr
Frau	Mrs
wie geht es Ihnen?	how are you?
danke	thank you
gut	very well

Dialog (Dialogue)

Herr Peters	Guten Tag!
Frau Meier	Guten Tag!
Herr Peters	Wie heißen Sie?
Frau Meier	Ich heiße Frau Meier.
	Wie heißen Sie?
Herr Peters	Ich bin Herr Peters.
Frau Meier	Wie geht es Ihnen?
Herr Peters	Danke, gut.
Frau Meier	Auf Wiedersehen!
Herr Peters	Auf Wiedersehen!

Übungen (Exercises)

1   Listen to the recording. Find the right picture for each phrase. (*Answers on page 126.*)

a)

b)

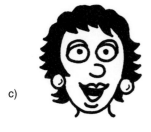

c)

d)

2 Make phrases with the words – use a separate sheet of paper if you need to. (*Answers on page 126.*)

1. | Herr | | ich | | Peters | | bin | .

2. | heißen | | wie | | Sie | ?

3. | Wiedersehen | | Auf | !

4. | Meier | | heiße | | Frau | | ich | .

5. | Tag | | Guten | !

6. | Sauer | | ich | | Herr | | heiße | .

7. | es | | geht | | Ihnen | | wie | ?

3 Listen to the recording. After each phrase, respond in German. (*Answers on page 126.*)

Tip (Hint)

There are some letters and sounds in German that you will not find in English. You have already learnt one of those letters – the **ß**. **ß** is sometimes written as **ss** and is called a 'sharp s'. Pronouncing it is easy – it's the same sound you make when saying 'hiss'!

Land und Leute

Germans are very polite. First names are only ever used for family and friends. Other people are always addressed as **Herr ...** (Mr) or **Frau ...** (Mrs) and as **Sie** – this is the polite form of 'you'. This means that even neighbours or work colleagues who have known each other for years will probably still call each other **Herr ...** and **Frau ...**!

Food and drink

In the restaurant/ordering drinks

Vokabular (Basic vocabulary)

ja bitte?	yes please?
und Ihre Frau?	and your wife?
ein Bier	a beer
ein Glas Wein	a glass of wine
Ihre Frau	your wife
Frau Ober!	waitress!
zu essen	to eat
zahlen, bitte!	the bill, please!
großes	large
kleines	small
weiß	white
rot	red
oder	or
nichts	nothing
nein	no
bitte sehr	please
danke	thank you

Dialog (Dialogue)

waitress	Ja bitte?
customer	Ein Bier, bitte.
waitress	Ein großes Bier?
customer	Nein, ein kleines Bier.
waitress	Und Ihre Frau?
customer	Ein Glas Wein.
waitress	Weiß oder rot?
customer	Weiß, bitte.
waitress	Ein kleines Glas?
customer	Nein – ein großes Glas.
waitress	Und zu essen?
customer	Nichts, danke.
waitress	Bitte sehr – ein Bier und ein Glas Wein.
customer	Danke. Frau Ober! Zahlen, bitte!

Übungen (Exercises)

1 Draw lines to match each question with the right answer. (*Answers on page 126.*)

1. Zu essen?

a) Nein – ein großes Glas.

c) Ein Bier, bitte.

b) Nichts, danke.

3. Ein kleines Glas?

2. Ja bitte?

2 Listen to the recording and put a cross by the right answers. (*Answers on page 126.*)

beer	wine		to eat
☐ small ☐ large	☐ red ☐ white	☐ small ☐ large	☐ yes ☐ no

3 You have to order for yourself and your husband. Listen to the recording and respond in the pauses, using the details below. (*Answers on page 126.*)

Tip (Hint)

You will have noticed that there are far more words beginning with a capital letter in German than in English. This is because all nouns (persons, animals or things) start with a capital letter.

But that's not all – there are other words in German beginning with a capital. You have already learnt one of those in the first unit – **Sie**, the polite form of 'you' which is used for everyone except family, children, very good friends and animals. For these you use another form, **du**.

Land und Leute

If you want to eat out, you will have no problems finding a **Restaurant** in Germany – but it helps if you know what signs to look out for! Restaurants are often called **Gasthof**, **Gasthaus** or **Gaststätte**. Or you could go to a **Lokal**, a **Wirtshaus** or a **Kneipe**. When you enter a German restaurant, you don't have to wait to be seated – you can choose any table you like!

U N I T 3 Shopping

Groceries

Vokabular (Basic vocabulary)

Guten Morgen	good morning
ein Brot	a/one (loaf of) bread
Obst	fruit
Äpfel	apples
ein halbes Pfund	half a pound
sechs Mark	six marks
haben Sie ...?	do you have ...?
wieviel?	how much?
was kostet das?	how much is that?
hier	here

Dialog (Dialogue)

customer	Guten Morgen!
assistant	Guten Morgen.
	Ja bitte?
customer	Ein Brot, bitte.
assistant	Ein Brot – bitte sehr.
customer	Und Obst. Haben Sie Äpfel?
assistant	Ja. Wieviel?
customer	Ein halbes Pfund, bitte.
assistant	Hier – ein halbes Pfund Äpfel.
customer	Was kostet das?
assistant	Sechs Mark.
customer	Sechs Mark – bitte.
assistant	Danke.
customer	Auf Wiedersehen.
assistant	Auf Wiedersehen!

Übungen (Exercises)

1 Find the words in the scrambled-up letters. (*Answers on page 126.*)

    1. SOBT   2. UNFDP   3. TRBO   4. PEÄLF

2 Listen to the recording. Put a cross by the right answer for each question. (*Answers on page 126.*)

    1. a) ☐ b) ☐   2. a) ☐ b) ☐   3. a) ☐ b) ☐   4. a) ☐ b) ☐

3 Now it's your turn. You are in a grocery store. Listen to the recording and respond to each phrase using the details opposite. (*Answers on page 126.*)

1.
2.
3.
4.
5.
6.
7.

Tip (Hint)

You have learnt your first plural word in this unit – **Äpfel**. Plurals (more than one) in German vary. Some words just add **-e** at the end – **Brot** becomes **Brote**. Other words add **-n** or **-en** as in **Frau** – **Frauen**. But there are no easy rules to follow – that's why the plural of **Apfel** is **Äpfel**! At this stage, try to remember the sound of the plural rather than its spelling, and limit yourself only to words that you might well need to use in the plural.

Land und Leute (Background)

A German pound – **Pfund** – is not the same as the English pound – it is slightly larger! The other thing to remember is that Germans do not use ounces, but grams (**Gramm**). There are 500 g (17,6 ounces) in a German **Pfund**, but only 454 g in an English pound. It is also very common to calculate prices in kilograms, so you will come across the German word **Kilogramm** quite often – just bear in mind that one **Kilogramm** is a bit more than two English pounds.

UNIT 4 Directions

Asking the way

wo ist ...?	where is ...?
ich verstehe nicht	I don't understand
gehen Sie	go
ich gehe	I go
dort ist	it's there
die Post	the post office
der Bahnhof	the station
da drüben	over there
geradeaus	straight on
links	left
rechts	right
dann	then
langsamer	more slowly
Entschuldigung	excuse me
ach so	I see

Dialog

man	Entschuldigung!
woman	Ja bitte?
man	Wo ist die Post, bitte?
woman	Die Post ist da drüben.
man	Wie bitte? Ich verstehe nicht.
woman	Die – Post – ist – da – drüben.
man	Ach so – danke. Und wo ist der Bahnhof?
woman	Gehen Sie geradeaus. Dann links – und dann rechts.
man	Entschuldigung – langsamer, bitte!
woman	Gehen Sie geradeaus – links – und rechts.
man	Ach, ich verstehe: Ich gehe geradeaus, dann links und dann rechts.
woman	Ja. Dort ist der Bahnhof.
man	Danke!
woman	Bitte sehr.

Übungen

1 Listen to the recording. Match up a) or b) to each phrase you hear.
(*Answers on page 126.*)

    1. a) Where's the railway station?
       b) Where's the train?
    2. a) Turn left!
       b) Turn right!
    3. a) Go straight on and left.
       b) Go straight on.

4. a) Where is there a letter box?
   b) Where is the post office?
5. a) Turn right and then left.
   b) Turn right and right again.

2 Listen to the dialogue on the recording. Select the correct maps. (*Answers on page 126.*)

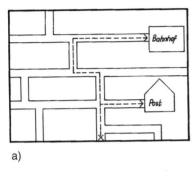

a)

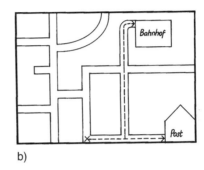

b)

3 Match up the German and English phrases. (*Answers on page 126.*)

1.	Ich verstehe nicht!	a)	Please/Don't mention it!
2.	Langsamer, bitte!	b)	More slowly, please!
3.	Entschuldigung!	c)	I don't understand!
4.	Wo ist der Bahnhof?	d)	Where is the railway station?
5.	Und wo ist die Post?	e)	And then straight ahead!
6.	Gehen Sie rechts!	f)	Excuse me!
7.	Und dann geradeaus!	g)	You go right!
8.	Bitte sehr!	h)	And where is the post office?

Tip

You will have noticed by now that there are different words in German for 'the': *der* **Bahnhof**, *die* **Post** or *das* **Rathaus**. The same goes for the German word for 'a': *ein* **Bahnhof**, *eine* **Post**, *ein* **Rathaus**. This is because the German equivalents of 'the' and 'a' depend on whether the noun they go with is masculine, feminine or neuter. Unfortunately there are few rules as to which gender a noun is – it's much easier to learn the gender as you learn a new word. Don't worry about this, though – you will almost always be understood even if you do make a mistake.

Land und Leute

When asking for directions in Germany, you, like the man in the dialogue in this unit, might not understand at first. Don't be afraid to try out your German phrases for 'I don't understand' or 'More slowly, please' – you will find everybody very helpful and patient and delighted to help foreign tourists.

UNIT 5 Numbers
Family

Vokabular

haben Sie Kinder?	do you have children?
wie alt?	how old?
wie alt sind sie?	how old are they?
... Jahre alt	... years old
ich habe	I have
Ihre Kinder	your children
meine Töchter	my daughters
mein Sohn	my son
einen Sohn	one son
Ihre Söhne	your sons
eins	one
zwei	two
drei	three
vier	four
fünf	five
sechs	six
sieben	seven
acht	eight
neun	nine
zehn	ten

Dialog

man	Guten Tag! Wie heißen Sie?
woman	Guten Tag. Ich heiße Meier – Anke Meier.
man	Haben Sie Kinder, Frau Meier?
woman	Ja, ich habe zwei Töchter – Anja und Meike – und einen Sohn, Lukas.
man	Wie alt sind Ihre Kinder?
woman	Anja ist sechs Jahre alt.
man	Und Meike?
woman	Meike ist neun Jahre alt. Und mein Sohn ist eins. Und Sie? Haben Sie Kinder?
man	Ja, ich habe zwei Söhne und drei Töchter.
woman	Wie alt sind Ihre Kinder?
man	Meine Töchter sind acht, sieben und vier Jahre alt.
woman	Und Ihre Söhne?
man	Tom ist fünf Jahre alt, und Daniel ist zehn.

Übungen

1 Listen to the recording. Put a cross by the number you hear. (*Answers on page 126.*)

1. a) ☐ 2   b) ☐ 8   2. a) ☐ 7   b) ☐ 9
3. a) ☐ 5   b) ☐ 3   4. a) ☐ 6   b) ☐ 10
5. a) ☐ 5   b) ☐ 4   6. a) ☐ 3   b) ☐ 7
7. a) ☐ 4   b) ☐ 10

2 Listen to the dialogues and fill in the grid. (*Answers on page 126.*)

daughters			sons		
how many?	names	age	how many?	names	age

3 Find the correct answers to the German questions. (*Answers on page 126.*)

1. Haben Sie Kinder?
2. Wie alt sind sie?
3. Haben Sie Söhne?
4. Wie alt sind sie?

a) Ja, ich habe vier Söhne.
b) Sie sind fünf, sechs, neun und zehn.
c) Katja ist sieben Jahre alt. Susi ist zwei Jahre alt.
d) Ja, ich habe zwei Kinder.

Tip

The words for 'my' and 'your' vary according to the gender (**der/die/das**) and number (singular/plural) of the noun following:

m(asculine)	*f(eminine)*	*plural (m or f)*
Ihr Mann	**Ihre Frau**	**Ihre Kinder**
mein Mann	**meine Frau**	**meine Kinder**

Look at these equivalents and try to learn them:

ich bin	I am
er/sie/es ist	he/she/it is
Sie sind	you are (*polite form*)
sie sind	they are

Land und Leute

When you are first introduced to German people, you might be surprised at the things they ask you. Germans are very direct, and apart from asking you about your family, they will probably want to know what your job is and how much you are earning, how big your house or flat is and how much rent you pay – and all this within the first hour of meeting you! Please do not be offended by these questions, though – German people consider them to be perfectly polite and acceptable within a conversation.

6 Public transport

Travelling by train

 ## Vokabular

kann ich Ihnen helfen?	can I help you?
wann fährt der Zug?	when does the train leave?
welches Gleis?	which platform?
der Fahrkartenschalter	the ticket office
zweimal nach Bremen	two tickets to Bremen
einfach	single
hin und zurück	return
um zwölf Uhr	at twelve o'clock
elf	eleven
zwölf	twelve
dreizehn	thirteen
vierzehn	fourteen
fünfzehn	fifteen
sechzehn	sixteen
siebzehn	seventeen
achtzehn	eighteen
neunzehn	nineteen
zwanzig	twenty

 ## Dialog

customer	Wo ist der Fahrkartenschalter? Ach, da drüben.
railway clerk	Ja bitte? Kann ich Ihnen helfen?
customer	Zweimal nach Bremen, bitte.
railway clerk	Einfach oder hin und zurück?
customer	Einfach, bitte. Was kostet das?
railway clerk	Siebzehn Mark und zwanzig, bitte.
customer	Bitte, hier. Wann fährt der Zug?
railway clerk	Um zwölf Uhr fünfzehn.
customer	Welches Gleis? Gleis vierzehn?
railway clerk	Nein, Gleis achtzehn. ... Ja bitte?
customer 2	Einmal nach Hamburg, bitte. Was kostet das?
railway clerk	Einfach kostet elf Mark. Hin und zurück kostet neunzehn Mark.
customer 2	Hin und zurück, bitte. Wann fährt der Zug?
railway clerk	Um dreizehn Uhr – Gleis sechzehn.

Übungen

1 Match each question below with the correct answer opposite. (*Answers on page 126.*)

4. Wann fährt der Zug?

1. Wo ist der Fahrkartenschalter?

2. Hin und zurück?

3. Welches Gleis?

b) (Dort drüben.)

c) (Nein, einfach.)

d) (Gleis sechzehn.)

a) (Um vierzehn Uhr.)

2 Listen to the two dialogues on the recording and fill in the grid. (*Answers on page 126.*)

	to	how many?	single/return	price	time	platform
1.						
2.						

3 Re-order the phrases below as if you were preparing your conversation about buying a ticket. (*Answers on page 126.*)

1. Welches Gleis?
2. Hin und zurück, bitte. Was kostet das?
3. Um 12 Uhr.
4. Einfach oder hin und zurück?
5. Achtzehn Mark.
6. Einmal nach Dortmund, bitte.
7. Hier, bitte. Wann fährt der Zug?
8. Gleis dreizehn.

Tip

There are a lot of very long words in German. Many are simply combinations of several words: **der Fahrkartenschalter** = **die Fahrkarten** (tickets) + **der Schalter** (counter). They always take the gender of the last component – here **der Fahrkarten*schalter*.**

Land und Leute

Travelling by train is a convenient and efficient mode of transport in Germany. The railway is called **Deutsche Bahn (DB)**. The main or central station is called **der Hauptbahnhof (Hbf)**. Other useful words: **die Auskunft** (information desk), **die Ankunft** (arrival), **die Abfahrt** (departure).

UNIT 7 Accommodation

At the hotel

Vokabular

Guten Abend	good evening
frei	vacant
ein Zimmer	a room
ein Einzelzimmer	a single room
ein Doppelzimmer	a double room
mit Bad	with a bath(room)
mit Dusche	with a shower
für eine Person	for one person
für zwei Personen	for two persons
mich	me
für eine Nacht	for one night
für zwei Nächte	for two nights
für wie viele?	for how many?

Dialog

customer	Guten Abend.
receptionist	Guten Abend. Kann ich Ihnen helfen?
customer	Ja. Haben Sie ein Zimmer frei?
receptionist	Ein Einzelzimmer oder ein Doppelzimmer?
customer	Ein Doppelzimmer, bitte.
receptionist	Mit Bad oder mit Dusche?
customer	Mit Bad.
receptionist	Und für wie viele Nächte?
customer	Für zwei Nächte.
receptionist	Für wie viele Personen?
customer	Für zwei – meine Frau und mich.
receptionist	Für zwei Personen – Zimmer 12.
customer	Danke.

Übungen

1 Match the phrases with the illustrations. (*Answers on page 126.*)

1. ein Einzelzimmer mit Dusche

a)   b)

2. für zwei Nächte

a)   b)

3. für zwei Personen

a) b)

4. ein Doppelzimmer mit Bad

a) b)

5. für eine Nacht

a) b)

2 Listen to the dialogues on the recording and fill in the grid. (*Answers on page 126.*)

customer	single	double	bath/shower	number of nights	room no.
1.					
2.					

3 Listen to the questions and, following the prompts, answer in the pauses on the recording. (*Answers on page 126.*)

Tip

The rules for the indefinite article 'a' **ein(e)** are almost the same as for **mein(e)** and **Ihr(e)**:

	m	n	f	pl (all genders)
a	**ein Mann**	**ein Hotel**	**eine Dusche**	**Zimmer***
my	**mein Mann**	**mein Hotel**	**meine Dusche**	**meine Zimmer****
your	**Ihr Mann**	**Ihr Hotel**	**Ihre Dusche**	**Ihre Zimmer****

* Note there is no plural for **ein** or **eine**.
** There is no plural ending for the word **Zimmer** – it stays just the same.

Land und Leute

Hotels in Germany can be called by several different names. The largest are **Hotels**, and many of these are similar to large hotels the world over. Smaller hotels are often called **Gasthof**. These are usually privately run and might have a small restaurant or bar. Smaller still is the **Pension**. These usually have no dining facilities. Hotels are always known by type first, name second – **Hotel Arabella**, **Gasthof Kern**.

Hobbies and pastimes

Nationalities/leisure time

Vokabular

woher kommen Sie?	where are you from?
kommen Sie aus Österreich?	are you from Austria?
was machen Sie gern?	what do you like doing?
ich komme aus ...	I come from ...
das ist in England	that's in England
ich bin Engländerin	I'm English (for a woman)
Amerikaner	American (for a man)
Deutsche	German (for a woman)
Engländerin	English (for a woman)
mein Hobby ist ...	my hobby is ...
meine Hobbys sind ...	my hobbies are ...
(das) Reisen	travelling
(das) Fernsehen	television
(der) Sport	sports
ich gehe gern ins Kino	I like going to the cinema
ich lese gern	I like reading
ich mag Filme	I like films

Dialog

Herr Klein	Guten Tag! Wie heißen Sie?
Frau Kahn	Guten Tag. Ich heiße Ellen Kahn.
Herr Klein	Woher kommen Sie? Sind Sie Deutsche?
Frau Kahn	Nein.
Herr Klein	Kommen Sie aus Österreich?
Frau Kahn	Nein, ich komme aus Peterborough. Das ist in England.
Herr Klein	Ach, Sie sind Engländerin?
Frau Kahn	Ja, ich bin Engländerin, und mein Hobby ist Reisen. Was machen Sie gern, Herr Klein?
Herr Klein	Ich gehe gern ins Kino. Ich mag Filme.
Frau Kahn	Und Sie, Herr Smith? Sind Sie Engländer?
Herr Smith	Nein. Ich bin Amerikaner.
Frau Kahn	Haben Sie Hobbys?
Herr Smith	Meine Hobbys sind Fernsehen und Sport. Und ich lese gern.

Übungen

1 Listen to the recording and mark the right answer for each phrase. (*Answers on page 126.*)

1. a) television and travelling ☐
   b) reading and films ☐
2. a) England ☐
   b) Austria ☐
3. a) travelling and films ☐
   b) reading and sports ☐

4. a) German ☐
   b) American ☐
5. a) cinema ☐
   b) reading ☐
6. a) Berlin (Germany) ☐
   b) London (England) ☐

2 Listen to the dialogue and fill in the grid. (*Answers on page 126.*)

	nationality	hobbies
Frau Klein		
Herr Williams		

3 Now it's your turn. Listen to the recording and make phrases with the information below. (*Answers on page 126.*)

1.

2.

3.

4.

Tip

Note that, when stating your nationality, you say the equivalent of 'I am Englishman' or 'I am German woman' – you do not use the word for 'a'. The endings to show gender follow a simple pattern except for one or two exceptions.

m	*f*	
Ich bin Engländer.	**Ich bin Engländerin.**	usual rule
Ich bin Amerikaner.	**Ich bin Amerikanerin.**	
Ich bin Deutscher.	**Ich bin Deutsche.**	exception

Land und Leute

The favourite pastimes in Germany are watching TV and reading, going to the cinema and doing sports.

 **Towns and villages**

Houses

Vokabular

haben Sie auch einen Garten?	do you have a garden as well?
wo wohnen Sie?	where do you live?
ich wohne	I live
es gibt nicht viel Verkehr	there isn't much traffic
nicht	not
es ist sehr ruhig	it's very quiet
sie hat	she/it has
in der Stadt	in town
auf dem Land	in the countryside
in einem Reihenhaus	in a terraced house
in einer Wohnung	in a flat
in einem Einfamilienhaus	in a detached house
eine Küche	a kitchen
ein Badezimmer	a bathroom

Dialog

Frau Klar	Wo wohnen Sie, Herr Schmidt?
Herr Schmidt	Ich wohne in der Stadt.
Frau Klar	Wohnen Sie in einem Reihenhaus?
Herr Schmidt	Nein, ich wohne in einer Wohnung.
Frau Klar	Wie viele Zimmer hat Ihre Wohnung?
Herr Schmidt	Sie hat vier Zimmer, eine Küche und ein Badezimmer.
Frau Klar	Ist Ihre Wohnung klein?
Herr Schmidt	Nein, sie ist sehr groß. Und Sie? Wo wohnen Sie?
Frau Klar	Ich wohne nicht in der Stadt – ich wohne auf dem Land.
Herr Schmidt	Wohnen Sie in einer Wohnung?
Frau Klar	Nein, ich wohne in einem Einfamilienhaus.
Herr Schmidt	Haben Sie auch einen Garten?
Frau Klar	O ja, ich habe einen großen Garten.
Herr Schmidt	Wohnen Sie gern auf dem Land?
Frau Klar	Ja, ich wohne gern auf dem Land. Es ist ruhig, und es gibt nicht viel Verkehr.

Übungen

1   Listen to the recording. Put a cross by the correct meaning for each phrase.
    (*Answers on page 126.*)
    1. a) I live in the city. ☐
       b) I live in the countryside. ☐
    2. a) My flat has three rooms, a kitchen and a bath. ☐
       b) My flat has two rooms and a kitchen. ☐
    3. a) Do you have a garden? ☐
       b) Do you have a kitchen? ☐
    4. a) I live in the countryside. ☐
       b) I live in the city. ☐
    5. a) Do you live in a detached house? ☐
       b) Do you live in a terraced house? ☐

2 Listen to the dialogue. Are the sentences true or false? (*Answers on page 126.*)

	true	false
1. Frau Kaiser lives in the countryside.	☐	☐
2. She lives in a detached house.	☐	☐
3. She has a big garden.	☐	☐
4. Herr Klein lives in the city.	☐	☐
5. His flat has two rooms, a kitchen and a bathroom.	☐	☐
6. He likes living in the city because it's quiet and there isn't much traffic.	☐	☐

3 Match the correct questions to the answers. (*Answers on page 126.*)

1. Wo wohnen Sie?
2. Wohnen Sie in einer Wohnung?
3. Wie viele Zimmer haben Sie?
4. Ist Ihr Haus klein?
5. Haben Sie auch einen Garten?
6. Wohnen Sie gern auf dem Land?

a) Ich habe sechs Zimmer, eine Küche und ein Badezimmer.
b) Nein, mein Haus ist sehr groß.
c) Ich wohne auf dem Land.
d) Ja, ich habe einen kleinen Garten.
e) Nein, ich wohne in einem Einfamilienhaus.
f) Ja, hier ist es sehr ruhig. Es gibt nicht viel Verkehr.

Tip

You already know the word for 'large' (**groß**) from previous units. Words like **groß** are called adjectives and they describe a noun. But have you noticed how the endings of adjectives and articles change in this unit?

ein groß*es* Bier – ein*en* groß*en* Garten

This is because articles and adjectives change depending on whether they go with a masculine, feminine or neuter noun. The rules for this are quite easy – you will learn more about this later. At this stage, just try to learn and practise the whole phrase rather than learning the words separately.

Land und Leute

Many Germans live in flats – living in a house is not as common as it is in other countries. And not all Germans own their property; many live in a rented flat or house all their lives. Rented property is almost always let unfurnished, and the tenants then decorate – and even carry out some structural changes – to their liking and with the permission of the landlord. When Germans say they live in a 'four room house', this does not mean four bedrooms but includes all other rooms apart from the kitchen, bathroom, toilet and utility room!

Weather

'What's the weather like?'

 ## Vokabular

wie ist das Wetter?	what's the weather like?
ist es kalt?	is it cold?
regnet es?	is it raining?
schneit es?	is it snowing?
es ist ...	it is ...
es regnet	it is raining
die Sonne scheint	the sun is shining
warm	warm
windig	windy
schlecht	bad
neblig	foggy
München	Munich

 ## Dialog

Frau Sauer	Sauer!
Herr Klein	Guten Tag, Frau Sauer, Klein hier – Herbert Klein.
Frau Sauer	Guten Tag, Herr Klein!
Herr Klein	Wie ist das Wetter in München, Frau Sauer?
Frau Sauer	Es ist sehr schön. Die Sonne scheint.
Herr Klein	Ist es kalt?
Frau Sauer	Nein, es ist nicht kalt. Es ist sehr warm.
Herr Klein	Ist es windig?
Frau Sauer	Nein, es ist nicht windig. Und wie ist das Wetter in Hamburg?
Herr Klein	Das Wetter ist schlecht. Es ist sehr kalt.
Frau Sauer	Regnet es?
Herr Klein	Ja, es regnet.
Frau Sauer	Schneit es?
Herr Klein	Nein, es schneit nicht, aber es ist neblig.

Übungen

 1 Listen to the phrases and put a cross by the right illustration for each phrase.
(*Answers on page 126.*)

1. a)   2. a)   3. a)   4. a)   5. a)

    b)   b)   b)   b)   b)

2 Listen to the dialogue and tick as many boxes as appropriate to describe the weather in Dortmund. Fill in the weather in Munich in English. (*Answers on page 126.*)

town	weather		
Dortmund	☐ good ☐ bad ☐ sunny ☐ snowy ☐ warm ☐ cold ☐ windy ☐ foggy ☐ rainy		
Munich			

3 Listen to the questions and respond using the information below. (*Answers on page 126.*)

1.

2. ~~COLD~~
WARM

3.

4. **BAD**
   COLD

Tip

Germans answer their phone either with just their family name (**Sauer!**) or they just give their telephone number. The person who has rung up then usually gives his or her name and adds **hier** – **Klein hier!** (it's Mr. Klein!). This may sound brusque or abrupt to you, but it is regarded as perfectly polite telephone manner.

At the end of the conversation, you should not say **Auf Wiedersehen!** (Good-bye!), but **Auf Wiederhören!** which means 'Speak to you soon' (lit. on hearing (from you) again).

Land und Leute

As in many other countries, the weather in the German-speaking countries varies a lot. It can become quite cold in the winter, especially in Southern Germany, Austria and Switzerland – there is almost always snow, and the temperature can be as low as minus 20°C (0°F). Summers are moderately warm, with temperatures in the mid-twenties on average (around 70°F). Northern Germany is known for its rain, and there are quite a lot of storms and storm tides on the Northern coast.

U N I T

Problems

At the chemist's

🎧 Vokabular

ich bin erkältet	I've got a cold
nehmen Sie die Tabletten	take the tablets
mein Kopf tut weh	my head hurts
sonst noch etwas?	anything else?
die Apotheke	the chemist (shop)
der Apotheker	the chemist (male)
die Kundin	the customer (female)
der Kunde	the customer (male)
die Medizin	the medicine
das Heftpflaster	the plaster
Halsschmerzen	sore throat
Kopfschmerzen	headache
Zahnschmerzen	toothache
dreimal	three times
pro Tag	a day

🎧 Dialoge

chemist	Ja bitte? Kann ich Ihnen helfen?
customer	Ja, ich bin erkältet. Ich habe Halsschmerzen.
chemist	Halsschmerzen? Ich habe Medizin für Sie. Sonst noch etwas?
customer	Ja, haben Sie Heftpflaster, bitte?
chemist	Hier, bitte sehr.
customer	Danke. Was kostet das?
chemist	Die Medizin – dreizehn Mark, und das Heftpflaster kostet vier Mark – siebzehn Mark, bitte.
chemist	Guten Tag! Ja bitte?
customer	Mein Kopf tut weh.
chemist	Sie haben Kopfschmerzen? Hier, ich habe Tabletten. Nehmen Sie die Tabletten dreimal pro Tag.
customer	Danke. Und meine Frau hat Zahnschmerzen.
chemist	Zahnschmerzen? Ich habe Medizin für Zahnschmerzen – bitte sehr.
customer	Danke schön. Was kostet das?
chemist	Die Medizin kostet elf Mark, und die Tabletten – acht Mark – neunzehn Mark, bitte.

Übungen

1   Look at the phrases and find the right picture for each one. (*Answers on page 126.*)

1. Ich habe Halsschmerzen!   a)   b)

2. Ich bin erkältet. a) b)

3. Mein Kopf tut weh. a) b)

4. Ich habe Zahnschmerzen. a) b)

2 Listen to the dialogue and answer the questions in English. (*Answers on page 126.*)

1. What does the customer complain of?
2. What does the chemist give him?
3. How often does he have to take the tablets?
4. What else does he buy?
5. What is his wife complaining of?
6. How much does he have to pay?

3 Use the following prompts to create your part in a likely conversation at the chemists. (*Answers on page 126.*)

1. yes – a cold
2. yes – sore throat
3. no – head hurts
4. yes, wife – toothache
5. plaster?
6. how much?

Tip

A verb is a 'doing' word which describes an action or a state (in English for example 'eat', 'remain', 'do'). In German the ends of the verbs change according to who is doing the action. This happens in English too, but less often (I eat → he eat*s*). Most verb endings in German follow a regular pattern, but many very common verbs do not (as in English). Here are the most frequently used forms of one such irregular verb, **haben** (to have):

ich ha*be* (I have)   **er/sie/es ha*t*** (he/she/it has)
wir ha*ben* (we have)   **Sie/sie ha*ben*** (you/they have)

Land und Leute

If you need to find a pharmacy in Germany, you need to look out for a sign saying **Apotheke**. In Germany **Apotheken** only sell medicinal products – if you need to find a chemist's for toiletries etc., you have to look for a **Drogerie**!

UNIT 12 The present, the future and the past

Arranging to meet this week

Vokabular

ich gehe ins Kino	I'm going to the cinema
treffen wir uns?	shall we meet?
wie wäre es mit Dienstag?	what about Tuesday?
am Montag geht es (nicht)	Monday is fine (no good)
diese Woche habe ich Zeit	I'm free this week
am Dienstag	on Tuesday
am Mittwoch	on Wednesday
am Donnerstag	on Thursday
am Freitag	on Friday
am Sonnabend/Samstag	on Saturday
am Sonntag	on Sunday
diese Woche	this week
ins Restaurant	to the restaurant
ins Theater	to the theatre

Dialog

Herr Klar	Guten Abend, Herr Müller. Diese Woche habe ich Zeit. Treffen wir uns?
Herr Müller	Ja, gern. Also – am Montag geht es nicht. Ich gehe ins Kino.
Herr Klar	Wie wäre es mit Dienstag?
Herr Müller	Nein, am Dienstag gehe ich ins Restaurant.
Herr Klar	Und am Mittwoch?
Herr Müller	Nein, am Mittwoch gehen meine Frau und ich ins Theater. Am Donnerstag geht es.
Herr Klar	Und am Freitag?
Herr Müller	Ja, am Freitag habe ich Zeit.
Herr Klar	Und am Sonnabend und am Sonntag?
Herr Müller	Nein, am Sonnabend und am Sonntag geht es nicht.
Herr Klar	Ja, wie wäre es mit Freitag?
Herr Müller	Ja. Wo treffen wir uns?
Herr Klar	Hier im Hotel, um achtzehn Uhr.

Übungen

1 Find the days of the week in the scrambled-up words. (*Answers on page 126.*)

1. MAGTON   2. GIRTEAF   3. EDSAGINT

4. GSENTORDNA   5. NAGSNOT   6. CTMOHIWT

2 Listen to the dialogue and, in English, fill in the diary for Frau Klein – what has she already planned, and what are she and Herr Kaiser now arranging to do when? (*Answers on page 126.*)

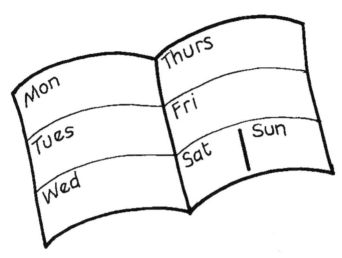

3 You are trying to meet up with friends. Go through your diary below and tell them in German whether you're free or what you're doing. (*Answers on page 126.*)

Monday	Tuesday	Wednesday	Thursday	Friday	Saturday	Sunday
can't do!	no – going to the cinema	no – we're going to the restaurant	no – can't do	no – we're going to the theatre	yes – free!	yes – free!

Tip

You can talk about the future using the present tense and a time expression: **Am Sonnabend gehe ich ins Kino** (On Saturday I am going to the cinema). Note that if there is a time expression first in the sentence, the verb (here **gehe**) comes next in the sentence and the subject (here **ich**) follows.

Land und Leute

In Germany shaking hands is an important part of being introduced and of saying hello and goodbye, both in formal and informal situations.

Self and others

Saying where you live

mein Name ist ...	my name is ...
ich kenne Basel gut	I know Basel well
wo wohnen Sie in der Schweiz?	where do you live in Switzerland?
Deutschland	Germany
Amerika	the United States
Kanada	Canada
Kanadier	Canadian (for a man)
Schweizerin	Swiss (for a woman)
Schottland	Scotland
eine schöne Stadt	a beautiful town
nicht wahr?	isn't it?
wie interessant!	how interesting!
auch	too

Dialog

Frau Sommer	Guten Tag! Sie sind Herr Taylor, nicht wahr?
Herr Taylor	Ja. Guten Tag. Mein Name ist Taylor – Chuck Taylor.
Frau Sommer	Und ich bin Gerta Sommer. Woher kommen Sie, Herr Taylor?
Herr Taylor	Ich komme aus Portland. Das ist in Amerika.
Frau Sommer	Ach, Sie sind Amerikaner! Mein Mann ist auch Amerikaner!
Herr Taylor	Wie interessant! Und Sie? Kommen Sie aus Deutschland?
Frau Sommer	Nein, ich komme aus der Schweiz – ich bin Schweizerin.
Herr Taylor	Wo wohnen Sie in der Schweiz?
Frau Sommer	Ich wohne in Basel.
Herr Taylor	Ach, ich kenne Basel gut. Basel ist eine schöne Stadt!
Frau Sommer	Und wie heißen Sie?
Herr Morris	Mein Name ist William Morris.
Frau Sommer	Woher kommen Sie, Herr Morris? Kommen Sie aus Schottland?
Herr Morris	Oh nein. Ich komme aus Toronto in Kanada. Ich bin Kanadier.

Übungen

1   Read Klaus Frank's description of himself. Then write a similar account – you are: Donna Miller, living in London, you're English, and your husband is American. (*Answers on page 126.*)

Ich bin Klaus Frank. Ich wohne in Dortmund. Ich bin Deutscher. Meine Frau ist Schweizerin.

2   Listen to the dialogue and fill in the grid. (*Answers on page 126.*)

	town	country/state
Herr Smith		
Frau Klein		

3   Now it's your turn. Listen to the recording. You will be asked to give your own name and say where you are from. After each phrase, respond in German using the following details for the remaining phrases.
(*Answers on pages 126–7.*)

1. your name is … (give your own name)
2. you live in … that's in … (your own town/country/state)
3. and you – are you from Germany?
4. ah, you're Swiss!
5. where do you live in Switzerland?
6. you know Bern well – Bern is a beautiful city

Tip

Note the following:

It is	**in Deutschland**
	in Österreich
	in England
	in Kanada
	in Schottland
but	**in *der* Schweiz**

And it is	**in Amerika**
but	**in *den* Staaten** (in the States)
or	**in den USA**

Land und Leute

Germany (**die Bundesrepublik Deutschland – BRD**) is divided into 16 counties – Bayern, Brandenburg, Baden-Württemberg, Mecklenburg-Vorpommern, Hessen, Niedersachsen, Nordrhein-Westfalen, Rheinland-Pfalz, Schleswig-Holstein, Sachsen, Sachsen-Anhalt, Thüringen, Saarland, Berlin, Hamburg, Bremen.

Until reunification in 1990, the Germans were divided into two nations: the **BRD** and the former **DDR (Deutsche Demokratische Republik)**. The largest county (**Bundesland**) is **Bayern** (Bavaria) in the South (70 555km^2); the smallest is **Bremen** in the North (404km^2). There are 80 million people living in Germany – 18 million of those live in the former East Germany. The capital of Germany is **Berlin**.

Food and drink

In the restaurant/paying the bill

Vokabular

Herr Ober	waiter
ein Schnitzel	a veal escalope
Pommes frites	French fries
eine Bratwurst	a fried sausage
eine Forelle	(a) trout
mit Kartoffelsalat	with potato salad
mit Gemüse	with vegetables
ein Mineralwasser	a mineral water
dazu	with that
oder?	*here:* wasn't it? *usually:* or
was macht das zusammen?	how much is that all together?
stimmt so!	keep the change!
einundzwanzig	twenty-one
zweiundzwanzig	twenty-two
dreißig	thirty
vierzig	forty
fünfzig	fifty
sechzig	sixty
siebzig	seventy
achtzig	eighty
neunzig	ninety
hundert	one hundred

Dialog

Frau Klein	Herr Ober! Zahlen, bitte!
waiter	Ja, gern. Also: eine Bratwurst mit Kartoffelsalat – 22 Mark.
Frau Klein	Und ein Mineralwasser.
waiter	Ein Mineralwasser – fünf Mark. 27 Mark. Und Ihr Mann?
Frau Klein	Eine Forelle mit Gemüse.
waiter	Eine Forelle mit Gemüse – 26 Mark. Und dazu ein Wein, oder?
Frau Klein	Ja, ein kleines Glas Wein.
waiter	Ein kleines Glas Wein – acht Mark, und 26 Mark – das sind 34 Mark.
Frau Klein	Was macht das zusammen?
waiter	61 Mark, bitte.
Frau Klein	Hier, 65 Mark – stimmt so.
waiter	Vielen Dank. Und Sie?
Herr Braun	Ein Schnitzel und Pommes frites.
waiter	25 Mark. Und ein großes Bier – sieben Mark. 32 Mark, bitte.
Herr Braun	Hier bitte – 35 Mark – stimmt so.
waiter	Vielen Dank.

1 Can you find seven words from this unit in the wordsquare? The words go from left to right and sometimes take two lines. (*Answers on page 127.*)

```
B R A T W U R S T G A
L M S C H N I T Z E L
C G E M Ü S E R Z J I
B M I N E R A L W A S
S E R A K Y T O P O M
M E S F R I T E S F U
W R F D B S P Y N E N
F O R E L L E R K N P
E A H C T R O B K A R
T O F F E L S A L A T
```

2 Listen to the dialogue on the recording and look at the two bills for each customer. Put a cross by the right bill. (*Answers on page 127.*)

1. a)　　　b)　　　　2. a)　　　b)

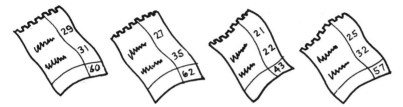

3 You have to pay for a meal for yourself and your wife. Listen to the recording and respond in German using the English prompts below. (*Answers on page 127.*)

1. You'd like the bill.
2. You had a fried sausage and French fries.
3. A veal escalope with potato salad.
4. A beer and a mineral water.
5. How much is that all together?
6. Here – 70 marks. Keep the change!

Tip

22 = 2 + 20 = **zweiundzwanzig**; 46 = 6 + 40 = **sechsundvierzig** etc.
Note **sechzig** (no **s** on **sechs***) and **siebzig** (not **sieben**).

Have you noticed the sound **ch** as in **mac*h*t**? Though not an English sound, you hear a very similar sound in the Scottish 'Loch'.

Land und Leute

On German menus you'll need to recognise **Vorspeisen** (starters), **Hauptspeisen** or **Hauptgerichte** (main meals) and **Nachspeisen** (desserts). **Getränke** are 'drinks'.

15 Shopping
Clothes

Vokabular

sie gefällt mir (nicht)	I (don't) like it
ich möchte	I would like
ich weiß nicht	I don't know
eine Jeans	a pair of jeans
die Kasse	the till
die Umkleidekabine	the changing room
diese	this
welche Größe?	which size?
passt	fits
teuer	expensive
kleiner	smaller
zu	too

Dialog

assistant	Guten Tag! Ja bitte?
customer	Guten Tag! Ich möchte eine Jeans.
assistant	Welche Größe?
customer	Ich weiß nicht – Größe 40 oder 42.
assistant	Jeans sind dort drüben … Hier, diese Jeans ist schön.
customer	Nein, sie ist zu teuer.
assistant	Und diese hier?
customer	Nein, sie gefällt mir nicht. Aber diese hier ist schön! Wo ist die Umkleidekabine, bitte?
assistant	Hier links … Passt die Jeans?
customer	Nein, sie ist zu groß.
assistant	Diese Jeans ist kleiner – Größe 38.
customer	Ja, diese Jeans passt! Was kostet die Jeans?
assistant	Diese Jeans kostet 98 Mark.
customer	Wo ist die Kasse, bitte?
assistant	Die Kasse ist dort drüben. Vielen Dank!

Übungen

1 Match the correct English version to the German sentences. (*Answers on page 127.*)

1. Die Jeans ist zu teuer.
   a) too expensive ☐
   b) too big ☐
3. Die Jeans ist zu klein.
   a) too small ☐
   b) too big ☐
5. Welche Größe?
   a) Which size? ☐
   b) How much? ☐

2. Wo ist die Kasse?
   a) Where are the changing rooms? ☐
   b) Where is the cash desk? ☐
4. Sie gefällt mir nicht.
   a) I don't like them ☐
   b) I like them ☐
6. Die Jeans passt.
   a) too small ☐
   b) fit perfectly ☐

2 Listen to the dialogue and put a cross by the right answers. (*Answers on page 127.*)

1. a) □ too small   b) □ too big   c) □ they fit

2. a) □ too small   b) □ too big   c) □ too expensive

3. a) □ too small   b) □ too big   c) □ they fit

4. a) □ too small   b) □ too big   c) □ they fit

3 Now it's your turn. Respond to the shop assistant in the pauses according to the illustrations below. The assistant begins the exchange. (*Answers on the recording and on page 127.*)

1. 2. 3.

4. 5. 6.

Tip

In this unit, you have learned how to say something is smaller or bigger instead of just small or big. The rules for this are very easy: all you do is add **-er** to the end of the adjective (**klein** – **kleiner**). If the adjective contains the letters **a**, **o** or **u**, you have to add an umlaut **ä**, **ö**, or **ü** as well. The umlaut changes the sound of the vowel on which it is placed. For example, **o** (as in 'broad') becomes **ö** (as the second 'e' in 'refer'): **groß** – **größer**.

Notice how you talk about **eine Jeans** = 'one pair of jeans' in the singular, not the plural. Similarly **eine Hose** – 'a pair of trousers', **eine Brille** – 'a pair of glasses'.

Note the expression **er/sie/es gefällt mir** – 'I like it' (literally 'it pleases me'). It's a handy one to remember!

Land und Leute

German shopping hours are not as flexible as they are in other countries. Most shops open at 9am and close at 6pm during the week. On most Saturdays, they are only open till 2pm (apart from the first Saturday in the month when shops are open till 4pm). And on Sundays, no shops are open at all!

Directions

'I'm looking for ...'

Vokabular

ich suche	I'm looking for
ich weiß es nicht	I don't know
es tut mir leid	I'm sorry
die Bank	the bank
die Straße	the street
bis zur Kreuzung	as far as the crossroads
bis zur Ampel	as far as the traffic lights
erste	first
zweite	second

Dialog

tourist	Entschuldigung?
passer-by	Ja? Kann ich Ihnen helfen?
tourist	Ja. Ich suche eine Apotheke.
passer-by	Eine Apotheke? ... Sie gehen bis zur Kreuzung.
tourist	Bis zur Kreuzung ...
passer-by	Ja. Dann nehmen Sie die erste Straße links.
tourist	Danke. Und wo ist eine Bank?
passer-by	Nehmen Sie die zweite Straße rechts. Gehen Sie bis zur Ampel.
tourist	Ich gehe die zweite Straße rechts – bis zur Ampel.
passer-by	Ja. Dort ist die Bank.
tourist	Und die Post? Wo ist die Post, bitte?
passer-by	Es tut mir leid, ich weiß es nicht.
tourist	Danke!

Übungen

1 Match up the phrases. (*Answers on page 127.*)

1. Sie gehen bis zur Ampel.
2. Die erste Straße links.
3. Ich gehe bis zum Bahnhof.
4. Ich suche eine Apotheke.
5. Ich suche die Bank.

a) I am looking for the chemist's.
b) I am looking for the bank.
c) I am going to the station.
d) Go as far as the traffic lights.
e) The first road on the left.

2 Listen to the recording and fill in the route on the maps. Do you end up at a), b) or c) each time? (*Answers on page 127.*)

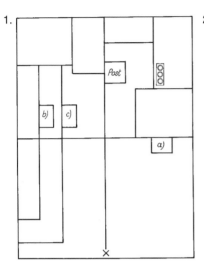
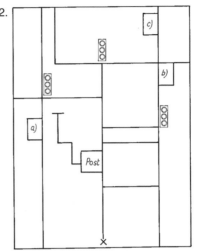

3 Listen to a number of different phrases in English. Say the equivalent in German in the pause. (*Answers on the recording and on page 127.*)

1. Excuse me!
2. I'm looking for the bank
3. go as far as the crossroads
4. take the first street on the right
5. go as far as the traffic lights
6. take the second street on the left

Tip

German commands or instructions are formed by simply putting the verb at the beginning of the sentence: **Sie – *gehen* – geradeaus** becomes ***Gehen* – Sie – geradeaus** and **Sie – *nehmen* – die erste Straße links** becomes ***Nehmen* – Sie – die erste Straße links**.

Land und Leute

In all the German-speaking countries, cars are driven on the right side of the road. When you are in a German (or a Swiss or Austrian) city or town, trying to find your way or to follow directions, please take extra care when you are crossing roads and streets. If you're used to the British system, it does take a while to remember that cars, buses and trucks are on the 'wrong' side of the road, and it is very easy to step into the path of a bicycle or motorbike speeding past!

Numbers

Telling the time

wann macht die Bank zu?	when does the bank close?
wie spät ist es?	what's the time?
wieviel Uhr ist es?	what's the time?
ich möchte Geld tauschen	I'd like to change some money
ich habe keine Zeit	I haven't got time
kommst du mit?	are you coming?
um wieviel Uhr beginnt der Film?	when does the film begin?
jetzt	now
Viertel	quarter
nach	past
vor	to
halb	half
Minuten	minutes
heute	today
nachmittag	afternoon
die Vorstellung	the show
gern geschehen!	you're welcome!

Dialoge

tourist	Entschuldigung!
passer-by	Ja bitte?
tourist	Ich möchte Geld tauschen. Wann macht die Bank zu?
passer-by	Um dreizehn Uhr.
tourist	Und die Post – wann macht die Post zu?
passer-by	Die Post macht heute um halb eins zu.
tourist	Wie spät ist es jetzt?
passer-by	Es ist Viertel nach zwölf – nein, es ist zwölf Uhr und siebzehn Minuten.
tourist	Vielen Dank.
passer-by	Gern geschehen!
Bettina	Guten Tag, Sven.
Sven	Guten Tag, Bettina. Ich gehe heute nachmittag ins Kino. Kommst du mit?
Bettina	Um wieviel Uhr beginnt der Film?
Sven	Um sechzehn Uhr.
Bettina	Nein, ich habe keine Zeit. Wir gehen heute nachmittag ins Theater.
Sven	Um wieviel Uhr beginnt die Vorstellung?
Bettina	Um Viertel vor vier. Wieviel Uhr ist es jetzt?
Sven	Es ist zwanzig nach zwölf.

Übungen

1 Read the **Tip** section on telling the time before you go any further. Then listen to the phrases on the recording and fill in the time for each phrase. (*Answers on page 127.*)

1.   2.   3.   4.   5.

2   Now it's your turn to tell the time. Look at the times below and say them out loud in German. (*Answers on the recording and on page 127.*)

1.   2.   3.

4.   5.   6.

3   Look at the times below. Write out each time in German. (*Answers on page 127.*)

1. 19:12
2. 09:10
3. 23:58
4. 16:55
5. 05:45
6. 07:30

Tip

Telling the time in German is not difficult. For most phrases you use an exact equivalent to the English:

es ist zwei Uhr	it is two o'clock
es ist zehn *nach* **zwei**	it is ten *past* two
es ist Viertel *nach* **drei**	it is quarter *past* three
es ist Viertel *vor* **drei**	it is quarter *to* three
but **es ist halb drei**	it is half *past* two

Remember the Germans use the twenty-four hour clock frequently when fixing business and social engagements. Here you give the hours first:

20.30 Uhr – zwanzig Uhr dreißig (8.30pm)

Land und Leute

In Germany banks are called **Bank** or **Sparkasse**. Shops do not accept traveller's cheques.

Public transport

Using public transport

Vokabular

Sie fahren am besten mit …	the best way is to take …
wie komme ich …?	how do I get …?
welcher Bus fährt …?	which bus goes …?
welche U-Bahn fährt …?	which tube goes …?
zum Flughafen	to the airport
der Flughafen	the airport
zum Bahnhof	to the station
mit dem Bus	by bus
mit der U-Bahn	by tube
die nächste Bushaltestelle	the nearest bus stop
die nächste U-Bahn-Station	the nearest tube station
Linie dreizehn	Number thirteen
um die Ecke	around the corner

Dialoge

passer-by	Ja bitte? Kann ich Ihnen helfen?
tourist	Ja, ich möchte zum Flughafen.
passer-by	Zum Flughafen? Sie fahren am besten mit dem Bus.
tourist	Welcher Bus fährt zum Flughafen?
passer-by	Linie dreizehn.
tourist	Wo ist die nächste Bushaltestelle, bitte?
passer-by	Gehen Sie hier links und dann die erste Straße rechts.
tourist	Vielen Dank.
tourist 2	Guten Tag. Wie komme ich zum Bahnhof, bitte?
passer-by	Sie fahren am besten mit der U-Bahn.
tourist 2	Welche U-Bahn fährt zum Bahnhof?
passer-by	Linie drei.
tourist 2	Wo ist die nächste U-Bahn-Station, bitte?
passer-by	Links um die Ecke.

Übungen

1 Form questions with these words. (*Answers on page 127.*)

1. zum   welcher   Flughafen   fährt   Bus ?

2. ich   wie   Bahnhof   komme   zum ?

3. die   ist   Bushaltestelle   wo   nächste ?

4. U-Bahn   zum   welche   Bahnhof   fährt ?

5. Ihnen   helfen   ich   kann ?

2 Listen to the recording. Are the sentences true or false? (*Answers on page 127.*)

	true	false
1. The woman wants to go to the station.	☐	☐
2. She has to take bus number 15.	☐	☐
3. The man has to take the tube.	☐	☐
4. The nearest tube is right and straight on.	☐	☐

3 Look at the English questions below and ask them out loud in German. (*Answers on page 127.*)

1. How do I get to the station, please?
2. Where is the nearest tube station?
3. Which bus goes to the airport?
4. Where is the nearest bus stop, please?
5. Which tube goes to the airport?
6. How do I get to the theatre?

Tip

Note these rules:

de*r* Bus → welche*r* Bus?

di*e* U-Bahn → welch*e* U-Bahn?

da*s* Gleis → welche*s* Gleis?

Land und Leute

Public transport is very developed in Germany. Apart from buses and tube trains, you will also find trams (**die Straßenbahn**) and suburban trains (**die S-Bahn**) in many German cities.

Local train services are also very widespread – a **Nahverkehrszug** (local train) will take you from a **Bahnhof** in the suburbs to the **Hauptbahnhof** in the centre of town.

Accommodation

Booking in advance

Vokabular

kann ich ein Zimmer reservieren?	can I book a room?
eine Übernachtung kostet …	one night is …
mit Fernseher	with TV
Halbpension	half board
Vollpension	full board
Frühstück	breakfast
im Juni	in June
nach Wien	to Vienna
vom zwölften bis zum fünfzehnten Juni	from 12 to 15 June
nur	only
also	that is
fünfhundert Schillinge	500 Schillings
eintausendfünfhundert Schillinge	1500 Schillings

Dialog

Frau Kant	Hotel Kant, guten Tag!
Herr Braun	Guten Tag!
Frau Kant	Wie kann ich Ihnen helfen?
Herr Braun	Ich komme im Juni nach Wien. Kann ich ein Zimmer reservieren?
Frau Kant	Ja, gern. Für wie viele Nächte?
Herr Braun	Vom zwölften bis zum fünfzehnten Juni, bitte.
Frau Kant	Also ein Zimmer für drei Nächte. Möchten Sie ein Einzelzimmer oder ein Doppelzimmer?
Herr Braun	Ein Einzelzimmer mit Dusche.
Frau Kant	Mit Fernseher?
Herr Braun	Ja bitte.
Frau Kant	Möchten Sie Halbpension oder Vollpension?
Herr Braun	Nein, nur Frühstück, bitte.
Frau Kant	Also, ein Einzelzimmer mit Dusche, Fernseher und Frühstück für drei Nächte.
Herr Braun	Ja. Was kostet das?
Frau Kant	Eine Übernachtung mit Frühstück kostet 500 Schillinge – das sind 1500 Schillinge.

Übungen

1 Write out these dates following the example in number 1. (*Answers on page 127.*)

(*Answers on page 127.*)

    1. 9.–11.6. vom neunten bis zum elften Juni
    2. 18.–19.6.
    3. 4.–8.7.
    4. 22.–23.8.

2 Listen to the dialogue and fill in the grid. (*Answers on page 127.*)

date	number of nights	room		price (total)
		☐ single	☐ breakfast	
		☐ double	☐ with a shower	
		☐ full board	☐ with a bath	
		☐ half board	☐ with TV	

3 Listen to the recording and use the information below to respond in German. (*Answers on page 127.*)

1. Can I book a room?
2. four nights
3. double room
4. with a shower + TV

Tip

These are the rules on changing numbers into dates:

1–3	**der erste, der zweite, der dritte**
4–19	**der vier*te*, der zehn*te*, der siebzehn*te*** etc.
20+	**der zwanzig*ste*, der dreißig*ste*** etc.

Land und Leute

As you know, Germany is not the only German-speaking country: there is **Österreich** (Austria) with its capital **Wien** (Vienna). German is also the main language of Switzerland (**die Schweiz**). The other languages spoken there are French, Italian and an ancient dialect, Rhaeto-Romanic.

HOTEL — CAFE - RESTAURANT

PATRIZIER

DAS HAUS MIT DER BESONDEREN NOTE

Moderne Fremdenzimmer
mit Bädern, Duschen, WC, Telefon TV
Kornhausstraße 25, 73525 Schwäbisch Gmünd
Telefon 0 71 71 / 3 04 34 + 6 63 03
Inh. Maria Theresia Baumhauer
Ständige Ausstellung, Malerei und Plastik
Geöffnet täglich von 6.30 Uhr bis 24.00 Uhr
Ruhetag für Café und Restaurant: Sonn- und Feiertage

DAS PELIKAN

Ihr Hotel in Schwäbisch Gmünd

Geschäftsführerin: Eva Rühle · 73525 Schwäbisch Gmünd · Türlensteg 9
Telefon 0 71 71 / 35 90 · Fax 0 71 71 / 35 93 59

Lassen Sie sich verwöhnen
in unseren neu gestalteten Räumlichkeiten!
Wir verfügen über 64 Zimmer
mit Bad/Dusche, WC, Fön, Radio, Minibar und Kabel-TV,
unser Gourmet-Restaurant
mit regionaler und internationaler Küche,
das Tagesbistro »P1«
und unsere gemütlich-rustikale »Erdinger-Quelle«.

Hobbies and pastimes

Leisure time

Vokabular

ich interessiere mich für ...	I'm interested in ...
ich finde Sport interessant	I find sports interesting
ich spiele Tennis	I play tennis
ich tanze	I dance
ich spiele gern Karten	I like playing cards
ich sehe	I see
wann beginnt ...?	when does ... start?
Kunst	the arts
Musik	music
in die Oper	to the opera
noch andere Hobbys	other hobbies
lieber	(to like) better
am liebsten	(to like) best
oft	often

Dialog

Frau Klein	Guten Abend, Herr Meier!
Herr Meier	Guten Abend, Frau Klein! Guten Abend, Herr Klein!
Herr Klein	Ach, ich sehe, Sie gehen ins Kino. Gehen Sie oft ins Kino?
Herr Meier	Ja, ich mag Filme. Ich gehe sehr gern ins Kino.
Frau Klein	Wann beginnt Ihr Film?
Herr Meier	Um achtzehn Uhr. Und Sie? Gehen Sie auch gern ins Kino, Frau Klein?
Frau Klein	Nein, ich gehe lieber ins Theater. Und ich interessiere mich für Kunst und Musik.
Herr Klein	Ja, ich auch – wir gehen oft in die Oper.
Herr Meier	Haben Sie noch andere Hobbys?
Herr Klein	Ich finde Sport interessant. Ich spiele am liebsten Tennis.
Frau Klein	Ich interessiere mich auch für Sport. Ich tanze gern.
Herr Klein	Und was machen Sie am liebsten, Herr Meier?
Herr Meier	Ich lese am liebsten. Und ich spiele gern Karten.

Übungen

1   Have a look at the **Tip** section before you start on the exercises. Look at the illustrations below. Circle the right illustration for each caption. (*Answers on page 127.*)

 = liking   = preferring    = liking most of all

1. Ich gehe am liebsten ins Kino.

   a) theatre   b) opera   c)  cinema

2. Ich lese gern.

   a) book   b)  cinema   c)  book

3. Ich spiele lieber Tennis.

a) 🙂 dancing   b) 🙂🙂 tennis   c) 🙂🙂🙂 tennis

4. Ich gehe am liebsten in die Oper.

a) 🙂 theatre   b) 🙂🙂 cinema   c) 🙂🙂🙂 opera

5. Ich spiele gern Karten.

a) 🙂 cards   b) 🙂🙂 book   c) 🙂🙂🙂 cinema

6. Ich lese am liebsten.

a) 🙂 book   b) 🙂🙂 book   c) 🙂🙂🙂 book

2 Listen to the dialogue on the recording. Are the sentences true or false? (*Answers on page 127.*)

	true	false
1. Frau Berger is going to the theatre.	☐	☐
2. The film starts at seven in the evening.	☐	☐
3. Herr Schmidt's hobby is music.	☐	☐
4. Watching TV is what he likes doing best.	☐	☐

3 Look at the prompts below and say them out loud in German. (*Answers on page 127.*)

1. your hobbies: music + football
2. you like going to the theatre most of all
3. you like going to the cinema better
4. ask 'what do you like to do best?'
5. ask 'do you have hobbies?'
6. ask 'are you going to the cinema?'

Tip

In this **Dialog**, you have heard how to say you like doing something better and most: **ich spiele *gern* Fußball – ich spiele *lieber* Fußball – ich spiele *am liebsten* Fußball**.

Here is another example: **Ich lese *gern*. Ich spiele *lieber* Tennis, aber ich gehe *am liebsten* ins Kino.** I like reading. I prefer playing tennis, but I like going to the cinema most of all.

Land und Leute

Germans love joining leisure clubs (**Vereine**). **Sportvereine** (sports clubs) are the most common, but all tastes are catered for with everything from **Schrebergartenvereine** (allotment clubs) to **Bauchtanzvereine** (belly-dancing clubs).

Towns and villages

Sights and amenities

was gibt es in Lübeck zu sehen?	what is there to see in Lübeck?
es gibt viel zu tun	there is a lot to do
das ist sehr praktisch	it's very convenient
wir wohnen	we live
eine schöne alte Stadt	a beautiful old town
viele Sehenswürdigkeiten	lots of sights
auf einem Bauernhof	in a farm house
der Bauernhof	the farm house
ein Stadtteil	a part of town
ein Dorf	a village
viele Geschäfte	many shops
das Geschäft	the shop
eine Kirche	a church
nördlich von	north of
südlich von	south of
zu viel	too much

Dialog

Herr Sauer	Wo wohnen Sie, Frau Meier?
Frau Meier	Ich wohne in Lübeck. Das ist eine kleine Stadt nördlich von Hamburg.
Herr Sauer	Was gibt es in Lübeck zu sehen?
Frau Meier	Also, Lübeck ist eine schöne alte Stadt. Es gibt viele Sehenswürdigkeiten – eine Kirche, alte Straßen ... Und wo wohnen Sie, Herr Sauer?
Herr Sauer	Ich komme aus Parching. Das ist ein Dorf südlich von München.
Frau Meier	Aah, Sie wohnen auf dem Land.
Herr Sauer	Ja, wir wohnen auf einem Bauernhof.
Frau Meier	Wohnen Sie gern in Parching?
Herr Sauer	Ja, sehr gern. Und Sie, Herr Smith? Wo wohnen Sie?
Herr Smith	Ich wohne in Fulham. Fulham ist ein Stadtteil von London.
Herr Sauer	Wohnen Sie gern in der Stadt?
Herr Smith	Ja, es gibt viel zu tun, und es gibt viele Geschäfte.
Herr Sauer	Das ist sehr praktisch, nicht wahr?
Herr Smith	Ja. Aber es gibt zu viel Verkehr!

Übungen

1 Make phrases with these words. (*Answers on page 127.*)

1. | viele | | es | | Sehenswürdigkeiten | | gibt | .

2. | Bauernhof | | auf | | ich | | einem | | wohne | .

3. | es | | Berlin | | was | | sehen | | gibt | | zu | | in | ?

4. | London | | Stadtteil | | ist | | Fulham | | ein | | von | .

5. | aus | | komme | | ich | | Parching | .

6. | Verkehr | | es | | zu viel | | gibt | .

7. | schöne | | Lübeck | | ist | | Stadt | | eine | | alte | .

2 Listen to the dialogue and fill in the details. (*Answers on page 127.*)

lives in	town/city
location	likes living there?
why/why not?	amenities

3 Look at the instructions below and listen to the questions in German. Answer in the pauses on the recording. (*Answers on page 127.*)

1. you live in Lübeck
2. no, that's a small town north of Hamburg
3. no, you live in a farm house
4. there are lots of sights – Lübeck is a beautiful old town

Tip

Have you noticed that the word for 'a' has taken on a new ending in this unit? **Ein Bauernhof** became **auf ein*em* Bauernhof** – in a farm house. This is because of the little word **auf**, a preposition. A preposition stands in front of a noun and links it to the rest of the sentence. But how do you know which ending goes with which noun (feminine, masculine and neuter)? The rules are simple:

> **ein/der Bauernhof** → **auf ein*em*/d*em* Bauernhof**
> **das Land** → **auf d*em* Land**

Land und Leute

70% of Germans live in towns or cities, and 30% live in the countryside. The three largest German cities are **München** (Munich), **Berlin** and **Hamburg**.

 **Weather**

Weather forecast

 Vokabular

die Wettervorhersage	the weather forecast
im Süden	in the south
im Norden	in the north
im Westen	in the west
im Osten	in the east
Grad	degrees
ein Gewitter	a thunderstorm
heiß	hot
sonnig	sunny
wolkig	cloudy
morgen	tomorrow

 Dialog

announcer Guten Tag, hier ist die Wettervorhersage.
Das Wetter heute: Im Süden ist es heiß und sonnig. 25 Grad.
Im Norden ist es kalt. Es ist wolkig, und es regnet. 18 Grad.
Im Westen gibt es ein Gewitter. Es ist sehr windig. 19 Grad.
Im Osten ist es warm und wolkig. 20 Grad.
Das Wetter morgen: im Süden: wolkig und windig.
Im Norden: kalt und neblig.
Im Westen: sonnig und warm.
Im Osten: heiß und Gewitter.

Übungen

 1 Listen to the phrases and mark the right picture for each phrase. (*Answers on page 127.*)

1. a)   b)   2. a)   b)

3. a)   b)   4. a)   b)

2 Listen to the weather forecast and fill in the grid in English. (*Answers on pages 127–8.*)

	weather	degrees
south		°
north		°
west		°
east		°

3 Form the German equivalents as in the example below. (*Answers on page 128.*)

1. Sunny in the south. 24 degrees. **Im Süden ist es sonnig. Vierundzwanzig Grad.**
2. Cloudy in the north. 19 degrees.
3. Thunderstorm in the east. 20 degrees.
4. Cloudy and windy in the west. 22 degrees.
5. Hot and windy in the south. 25 degrees.
6. Rainy in the north. 18 degrees.

Tip

In the previous unit, you learned how the word for 'a' – **ein(e)** – changes depending on the preposition **in** that goes with it.

In this unit, you have learned another new word: **im (im Süden, im Norden ...)**. But **im** is not really a new word – it is the short form of **in dem**: *in dem* Süden simply becomes *im* **Süden**!

Land und Leute

To convert from Fahrenheit to Centigrade (Celsius), subtract 32 and multiply by $\frac{5}{9}$:

°F	°C
0	−17.8
32	0
50	10
70	21.1
90	32.2

 **Problems**

Feeling ill/at the doctor's

was fehlt Ihnen?	what's wrong?
wo tut es weh?	where does it hurt?
trinken Sie viel Wasser!	drink lots of water!
essen Sie nichts!	don't eat anything!
bleiben Sie im Bett!	stay in bed!
kommen Sie morgen wieder!	come back tomorrow!
Frau Doktor	doctor (woman)
Bauchschmerzen	stomach ache
Durchfall	diarrhoea
Grippe	flu
ein Rezept	a prescription
Husten	cough

Dialoge

doctor	Guten Tag, was fehlt Ihnen?
patient	Guten Tag, Frau Doktor. Ich habe Bauchschmerzen.
doctor	Haben Sie Durchfall?
patient	Ja, ich habe auch Durchfall.
doctor	Hier ist ein Rezept. Trinken Sie viel Wasser!
patient	Danke.
doctor	Essen Sie nichts, und bleiben Sie im Bett!
patient	Ja. Auf Wiedersehen!
patient 2	Guten Tag, Frau Doktor.
doctor	Guten Tag. Wo tut es weh?
patient 2	Ich habe Husten. Mein Hals tut weh, und mein Kopf tut weh.
doctor	Sie haben Grippe. Nehmen Sie diese Tabletten dreimal pro Tag.
patient 2	Danke sehr.
doctor	Kommen Sie morgen wieder!
patient 2	Ja. Auf Wiedersehen.

Übungen

1 Put a cross by the right illustration for each phrase. (*Answers on page 128.*)

1. Bleiben Sie im Bett!

 a)   b)

2. Sie haben Grippe.

 a)   b)

3. Essen Sie nichts!

a) b)

4. Trinken Sie viel Wasser!

a) b)

2 Listen to the dialogue. Fill in the details. (*Answers on page 128.*)

illness/complaint	medication
	doctor's orders
how often?	

3 You are at the doctor's. Look at the list of illnesses below. Give the equivalents in German. (*Answers on page 128.*)

1. I have a stomach ache
2. I have got flu
3. my head hurts
4. I've got diarrhoea
5. I have a cough
6. my throat hurts

Tip

Verbs like **trinken, bleiben** and **kommen** are all regular verbs – their endings follow a regular pattern:

trinken (to drink)			
ich	**trinke**		
du	**trinkst**	**wir**	**trinken**
er/sie/es	**trinkt**	**Sie/sie**	**trinken**

Note that **wir, Sie** and **sie** (pl.) all have the same ending.

Land und Leute

If you just need to go to a GP during your visit to Germany, you have to look for a **Allgemeinarzt** or **praktischer Arzt**. All German doctors display their name, title and their opening hours outside their practices. If you have to go to the hospital, you have to ask for **das Krankenhaus**. And if you're looking for the casualty department, you need to find **die Unfallabteilung** – but hopefully you will stay healthy and have no accidents while you're away!

24 The present, the future and the past

Arranging to meet tomorrow

Vokabular

was machen Sie?	what are you doing?
was machen wir?	what shall we do?
wollen wir essen gehen?	shall we go for a meal?
kommen Sie mit?	are you coming?
am Sonnabend habe ich frei	on Saturday I'm free
ich spiele Federball	I play badminton
ich spiele Fußball	I play football
sagen wir	let's say
ins Sportstudio	to the sports centre
heute Abend	this evening
vielleicht	maybe

Dialog

Frau Klein   Was machen Sie heute Abend, Herr Sommer?
Herr Sommer   Ich gehe ins Kino. Und Sie? Was machen Sie heute Abend?
Frau Klein   Ich gehe ins Sportstudio – ich spiele dort Federball. Was machen Sie morgen?
Herr Sommer   Ich spiele Fußball. Was machen Sie am Sonnabend?
Frau Klein   Am Sonnabend habe ich frei. Treffen wir uns?
Herr Sommer   Ja, gern. Was machen wir?
Frau Klein   Wollen wir essen gehen?
Herr Sommer   Ja. Wo treffen wir uns?
Frau Klein   In der Stadt vielleicht?
Herr Sommer   Ja, und Sie, Herr Smith? Kommen Sie mit?
Herr Smith   Ja, gern. Wann treffen wir uns?
Frau Klein   Sagen wir um neunzehn Uhr?
Herr Smith   Ja. Auf Wiedersehen! Bis Sonnabend!

Übungen

1   Mark the right answer for each question. (*Answers on page 128.*)

1. Wo treffen wir uns?   a) Am Sonnabend.   b) In der Stadt.

2. Wann treffen wir uns?   a) In der Stadt.   b) Um neunzehn Uhr.

3. Was machen wir?   a) Ja, gern.   b) Wir gehen ins Restaurant.

2   Listen to the dialogues. Are the sentences true or false? (*Answers on page 128.*)

	true	false
1.		
a) Herr Kaiser is going to the cinema this evening.	☐	☐
b) Frau Schneider has nothing planned for the following evening.	☐	☐
c) They arrange to go to the cinema.	☐	☐
d) They arrange to meet in town at six o'clock.	☐	☐
2.		
a) Herr and Frau Klein are going to the restaurant this evening.	☐	☐
b) They arrange to meet Mr. Smith on Saturday.	☐	☐
c) They arrange to go to the theatre.	☐	☐
d) They agree to meet at six o'clock.	☐	☐

3   Listen to the phrases and reply using the information below. (*Answers on page 128.*)

1. cinema – what are you doing this evening?
2. what are you doing tomorrow?
3. Saturday free – shall we meet?
4. shall we go to the theatre?
5. in town – when shall we meet?

Tip

Questions which only need **ja** or **nein** as an answer are formed like this:

> **Wir *treffen* uns.**   →   ***Treffen* wir uns?**

To get more information, add a question word at the beginning of the sentence:

***Wann* treffen wir uns?**	**Wann?**	When?
***Wo* treffen wir uns?**	**Wo?**	Where?
***Was* machen wir?**	**Was?**	What?
***Wie* geht es Ihnen?**	**Wie?**	How?
***Wieviel* kostet das?**	**Wieviel?**	How much?

Land und Leute

Other greetings:

In Southern Germany/Austria: **Grüß Gott!** (Good morning/afternoon/evening)
Northern Germany: **Tschüs** (informal good-bye)

 **Self and others**

'May I introduce . . . ?'

 ## Vokabular

darf ich vorstellen?	may I introduce?
wohin gehen Sie?	where are you going?
welcher Film läuft?	which film is being shown?
ich muss mich beeilen	I have to hurry
ich weiß	I know
lass uns schwimmen gehen!	let's go swimming!
lass uns fernsehen!	let's watch TV!
ich möchte ins Kino gehen	I'd like to go to the cinema
Otto-Filme mag ich nicht	I don't like Otto films
mein Freund	my boyfriend/male friend
meine Freundin	my girlfriend/female friend
mit meiner Freundin	with my girlfriend/female friend
angenehm	delighted (to meet you)
lustig	funny
von	by/from

 ## Dialog

Herr Klein	Guten Tag, Frau Meier! Wie geht es Ihnen?
Frau Meier	Guten Tag, Herr Klein! Danke, gut! Darf ich vorstellen: mein Freund, Andi Klose.
Herr Klein	Guten Tag, Herr Klose! Angenehm!
Herr Klose	Guten Tag, Herr Klein!
Frau Meier	Wohin gehen Sie, Herr Klein?
Herr Klein	Ich gehe mit meiner Freundin in die Oper. Oh, ich muss mich beeilen – die Vorstellung beginnt um zwanzig Uhr. Auf Wiedersehen!
Herr Klose	So, was machen wir jetzt?
Frau Meier	Ich weiß – lass uns schwimmen gehen!
Herr Klose	Nein, es ist zu kalt. Ich möchte lieber ins Kino gehen.
Frau Meier	Ja, gut. Welcher Film läuft?
Herr Klose	Der neue Film von Otto. Er ist sehr lustig!
Frau Meier	Nein, Otto-Filme mag ich nicht. Lass uns lieber fernsehen!
Herr Klose	Ja gut – lass uns fernsehen!

Übungen

1 Make phrases with the words. (*Answers on page 128.*)

1. | vorstellen | | ich | | darf | ?

2. | mich | | beeilen | | muss | | ich | .

3. | schwimmen | | uns | | gehen | | lass | !

4. | möchte | | ins | | Kino | | ich | | gehen | | lieber | .

2 Listen to the dialogue on the recording. Answer the questions below in English. (*Answers on page 128.*)

1. Whom does Frau Kaiser introduce to Herr Sauer?
2. Where are the two women going?
3. What time does the film start?

3 Practise saying these phrases in German. (*Answers on page 128.*)

1. let's go into town
2. yes, fine; which film is showing?
3. the film is very funny
4. I have to hurry – I'm going to the theatre
5. the show starts at half past eight

Tip

If you only want to negate one particular word, the word for 'not' – **nicht** – goes in front *of this word:*

| Ich gehe in die Oper. | Ich gehe *nicht* in die Oper. |

If you want to negate a whole sentence or phrase, the **nicht** goes at the end of that sentence:

| Otto-Filme mag ich. | Otto-Filme mag ich *nicht*. |

Land und Leute

Special dialects are still spoken in various parts of the German-speaking countries, but **Hochdeutsch** (the standard German) is of course the main spoken German. Many people have regional accents, but these are generally not too difficult to understand.

Food and drink

In a café

eine Tasse Tee	a cup of tea
ein Kännchen Kaffee	a pot of coffee
mit Milch	with milk
mit Zucker	with sugar
ohne Zitrone	without lemon
ein Stück	a piece of
Apfelstrudel	apple strudel
Käsekuchen	cheesecake
Schokoladentorte	chocolate gateau
ohne Sahne	without cream
kommt sofort!	it's on its way!

Dialog

customer	Herr Ober! Ich möchte eine Tasse Tee, bitte.
waiter	Mit Zitrone?
customer	Nein, ohne Zitrone. Mit Milch und Zucker, bitte.
waiter	Und Sie?
customer 2	Ein Kännchen Kaffee, bitte.
waiter	Mit Milch?
customer 2	Nein, ohne Milch. Und ein Stück Apfelstrudel.
waiter	Ein Stück Apfelstrudel mit Sahne?
customer 2	Nein, ohne Sahne.
waiter	Gern. Und Sie?
customer	Haben Sie Käsekuchen?
waiter	Nein, Käsekuchen haben wir nicht.
customer	Dann nehme ich ein Stück Schokoladentorte.
waiter	Also: eine Tasse Tee mit Milch und Zucker, ein Kännchen Kaffee ohne Milch, ein Stück Apfelstrudel und ein Stück Schokoladentorte – kommt sofort!

Übungen

1 Put a cross by the right illustration for each phrase. (*Answers on page 128.*)

1. Eine Tasse Tee mit Zucker und Zitrone.

a)   b)

2. Eine Stück Apfelstrudel ohne Sahne.

a)   b)

3. Ein Kännchen Kaffee mit Milch und ohne Zucker.

a)   b)

4. Ein Stück Käsekuchen mit Sahne.

a)   b)

2 Listen to the dialogue and fill in the grid in English. (*Answers on page 128.*)

	to drink	with	to eat	with
customer 1				
customer 2				

3 You are in a café ordering cakes and drinks for your family. Listen to the waitress' questions on the recording and respond using the information in the illustrations below. (*Answers on page 128.*)

to drink   to eat

1. 2. 3. 4. 5. 6. 7.

Tip

In Unit 23, you learned the rules for regular verbs. Irregular verbs don't follow that pattern in the **du** and **er/sie/es** form – some letters are added, left out or changed:

fahren (to drive, go)	**sehen** (to see, watch)	**essen** (to eat)
ich fahre	ich sehe	ich esse
du f**ä**hrst	du si**e**hst	du *iss*t
er f**ä**hrt	er si**e**ht	er *iss*t
a → ä	e → ie	e → i

Land und Leute

Germans love their afternoon **Kaffee und Kuchen** (coffee and cakes), so you will have no problem finding a **Konditorei** or **Café**. It is customary in German coffee and cake shops to select your cake or gateau from the counter display before you sit down at a table.

Shopping

In the department store

Vokabular

ich suche …	I'm looking for …
wo finde ich Zeitschriften?	where do I find magazines?
Bücher	books
Filme	films
Geschenke	gifts
die Geschenkabteilung	the gifts department
Schreibwaren	stationery
neben den Süßwaren	next to the confectionery
im ersten Stock	on the first floor
im zweiten Stock	on the second floor
im Erdgeschoss	on the ground floor
im Untergeschoss	in the basement
die Rolltreppe	the escalator
der Fahrstuhl	the lift

Dialoge

customer	Entschuldigung! Ich suche Bücher.
assistant	Bücher sind im ersten Stock.
customer	Danke. Und wo finde ich Zeitschriften?
assistant	Zeitschriften sind im Erdgeschoss – dort drüben links.
customer	Und Filme – wo finde ich Filme?
assistant	Filme sind im Untergeschoss.
customer	Vielen Dank. Wo ist die Rolltreppe, bitte?
assistant	Gehen Sie links und dann immer geradeaus. Dort ist die Rolltreppe.
customer 2	Entschuldigung! Ich suche Geschenke. Wo ist die Geschenkabteilung?
assistant	Die Geschenkabteilung? Geschenke sind im zweiten Stock.
customer 2	Danke. Wo ist der Fahrstuhl, bitte?
assistant	Der Fahrstuhl ist dort rechts.
customer 2	Und wo finde ich Schreibwaren?
assistant	Schreibwaren sind hier im Erdgeschoss – neben den Süßwaren. Sie gehen links und dann rechts.
customer 2	Vielen Dank!

Übungen

1 Put a cross by the right translation for each phrase. (*Answers on page 128.*)

1. Wo finde ich Zeitschriften, bitte?
   a) Do you have magazines, please?
   b) Where can I find magazines please?

2. Geschenke sind im Erdgeschoss.
   a) Presents are on the ground floor.
   b) Presents are in the basement.

3. Entschuldigung! Ich suche Schreibwaren.
   a) Excuse me! I'm looking for stationery.
   b) Excuse me! I'm looking for the lift.

4. Der Fahrstuhl ist dort rechts.
   a) The lift is over there on the right.
   b) The escalator is over there on the right.

5. Wo finde ich die Rolltreppe?
   a) Where can I find the gifts department?
   b) Where can I find the escalator?

2 Listen to the dialogue and fill in the store plan. (*Answers on page 128.*)

KAUFHAUS
3. St.
2. St.
1. St.
E
U

3 Now it's your turn – you're in the department store asking a sales assistant the questions below in German. The assistant will start by greeting you. (*Answers on the recording and on page 128.*)

1. Where do I find books, please?
2. Excuse me, I'm looking for stationery.
3. Where do I find films, please?
4. Where is the gifts department, please?
5. Excuse me – where do I find magazines, please?
6. Where is the escalator, please?

Tip

Here are some more plurals:

die Zeitschrift	**das Geschenk**	**der Film**	**das Buch**
die Zeitschrift*en*	*die* Geschenk*e*	*die* Film*e*	*die* B*ücher*

Note that the plural of **der/die/das** is the same for all plural words – **die**.

Land und Leute

The major German department stores (**das Kaufhaus**) are **Karstadt** and **Horten**. You will also find large shopping centres (**das Einkaufszentrum**) and shopping arcades (**die Einkaufspassage**) throughout the German-speaking countries, so why don't you take the opportunity to browse – and maybe to shop – in one of those stores during your visit!

Directions

By car

Vokabular

wie komme ich zum Flughafen?	how do I get to the airport?
wie weit ist es bis . . .?	how far is it to . . .?
die Bundesstraße	the federal road/A road
die Autobahn	the motorway
die Landstraße	the country road
die nächste Tankstelle	the next petrol station
fünfhundert Meter	five hundred metres
auf der linken/rechten Seite	on the left/right-hand side
am besten	the best way
ungefähr	approximately
zweihundert	two hundred
dreihundert	three hundred
vierhundert	four hundred
fünfhundert	five hundred
sechshundert	six hundred
siebenhundert	seven hundred
achthundert	eight hundred
neunhundert	nine hundred

Dialog

tourist	Entschuldigung! Wie komme ich zum Flughafen?
passer-by	Zum Flughafen? Sie fahren fünfhundert Meter geradeaus bis zur großen Kreuzung. Dann nehmen Sie die Landstraße … nein, Sie nehmen die Bundesstraße 2.
tourist	Fünfhundert Meter geradeaus – dann die Bundesstraße 2.
passer-by	Ja. Dann nehmen Sie die Autobahn 1 bis zum Flughafen.
tourist	Wie weit ist es bis zum Flughafen?
passer-by	Ungefähr dreißig Kilometer.
tourist	Danke. Und wo ist die nächste Tankstelle?
passer-by	Fahren Sie an der Ampel rechts. Die Tankstelle ist auf der linken Seite.

Übungen

1 Fill in the gaps with the words below. (*Answers on page 128.*)

Autobahn	nächste	zweihundert	Richtung

1. Fahren Sie in _____ Hamburg.

2. Sie nehmen am besten die _____.

3. Wo ist die _____ Tankstelle?

4. Sie fahren _____ Meter geradeaus.

2 Listen to the recording. Are the phrases true or false?
(*Answers on page 128.*)

	true	false
1. The tourist wants to get to the station.	☐	☐
2. He has to drive straight on for 500 metres and then has to take the federal road 10.	☐	☐
3. After that, he has to drive for 25 kilometres and then has to take the motorway 6.	☐	☐
4. The airport is 15 kilometres away.	☐	☐
5. The petrol station is left at the lights – it's on the right-hand side.	☐	☐

3 Now it's your turn to ask for direction. Form questions in German with the information below. (*Answers on page 128.*)

1. Excuse me – how do I get to the airport?
2. How far is it to the airport?
3. How do I get to motorway 1?
4. What's the best way to get to Bremen?
5. Where is the nearest petrol station?

Tip

Numbers over a hundred are formed by simply adding the two sets of numbers together: 150 = 100 + 50 = **einhundert(und)fünfzig**. The **und** is often dropped:

201 = **zweihundert(und)eins**

462 = **vierhundert(und)zweiundsechzig** etc.

Land und Leute

German roads and motorways are very comfortable to travel on, and almost all towns are connected by a dense net of motorways.

You do not have to pay a toll on German motorways, but you do have to in Switzerland.

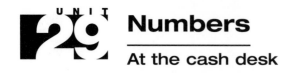

Numbers

At the cash desk

Vokabular

das macht zusammen	the total is
ich zahle bar	I'm paying cash
Sie bekommen eine Mark zurück	your change is one Mark
wie möchten Sie bezahlen?	how would you like to pay?
Euroschecks	euro cheques
Kreditkarten	credit cards
Pfennig	pence
das blaue Hemd	the blue shirt
das grüne Kleid	the green dress
die braunen Schuhe	the brown shoes

Dialoge

customer	Entschuldigen Sie bitte! Ich suche die Kasse.
assistant	Die Kasse ist dort drüben um die Ecke.
customer	Danke. ... Guten Tag.
assistant 2	Guten Tag. Also – das blaue Hemd kostet fünfunddreißig Mark. Und die braunen Schuhe kosten dreiundsechzig Mark und sechzig Pfennig. Das macht zusammen achtundneunzig Mark und sechzig Pfennig.
customer 2	Achtundneunzig Mark und sechzig Pfennig?
assistant 2	Ja. Wie möchten Sie bezahlen?
customer 2	Ich zahle bar. Hier bitte – hundert Mark.
assistant 2	Danke. Sie bekommen eine Mark und vierzig Pfennig zurück.
customer 3	Guten Tag!
assistant 2	Guten Tag. Das grüne Kleid – zweiundvierzig Mark. Wie möchten Sie bezahlen?
customer 2	Nehmen Sie Kreditkarten?
assistant 2	Nein, leider nicht.
customer 2	Nehmen Sie Euroschecks?
assistant 2	Ja, wir nehmen Euroschecks.

Übungen

1 Match the right price tag to each sentence. (*Answers on page 128.*)

1. Die Jeans kostet vierundfünfzig Mark. a) DM 54.– b) DM 43.–

a) DM 97.– b) DM 79.– 2. Die Schuhe kosten neunundsiebzig Mark.

3. Das Hemd kostet dreiunddreißig Mark. a) DM 32.– b) DM 33.–

a) DM 57.– b) DM 65.– 4. Das T-Shirt kostet fünfundsechzig Mark.

2 Listen to the dialogue and fill in the grid below. (*Answers on page 128.*)

	item	price	method of payment
1.			
2.			
3.			
		total =	

3 You are paying for your purchases at the cash desk. The cashier asks you to tell her the prices of each item. Reply in the pauses in complete sentences using the information below. (*Answers on page 128.*)

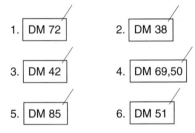

1. DM 72   2. DM 38

3. DM 42   4. DM 69,50

5. DM 85   6. DM 51

Tip

You've already learned in Unit 9 that adjectives describe nouns (a person, animal or thing). Colours for example are adjectives. Notice these rules:

masculine	**der braune Rock**
feminine	**die blaue Jeans**
neuter	**das grüne Kleid**
plural	**die braunen Schuhe**

Land und Leute

Germans prefer to pay by cash – especially in shops and supermarkets. There is a baffling variety of different bank notes available in Germany – the largest being **1000 Mark** (approx. £400)! Cheques are mainly used for business transactions, but hardly ever at the check-out counter – Germans find this method of payment very unusual and inconvenient. And although credit cards are becoming more and more widespread, the majority of Germans would never use them for everyday purchases.

 **Public transport**

Changing and getting off

Vokabular

muss ich umsteigen?	do I have to change?
wo muss ich aussteigen?	where do I have to get off?
was kostet eine Fahrkarte?	how much is a ticket?
wo kaufe ich Fahrkarten?	where do I buy tickets?
Sie müssen in Hannover umsteigen	you have to change in Hanover
Sie müssen am Martinsplatz aussteigen	you have to get off at the Martinsplatz
Fahrkarten bekommen Sie an der Haltestelle	you'll get tickets at the stop
die S-Bahn	the suburban train
zum Bahnhof	to the station
erster Klasse	first class
zweiter Klasse	second class

 ### Dialoge

tourist	Entschuldigen Sie bitte! Welcher Bus fährt zum Bahnhof?
passer-by	Zum Bahnhof? Sie nehmen am besten die S-Bahn Linie 6.
tourist	Danke. Und wo muss ich aussteigen, bitte?
passer-by	Sie müssen am Martinsplatz aussteigen.
tourist	Vielen Dank! Und wo kaufe ich Fahrkarten?
passer-by	Fahrkarten bekommen Sie an der Haltestelle.
tourist	Danke schön!
clerk	Ja bitte?
tourist	Was kostet eine Fahrkarte nach Hamburg?
clerk	Einfach oder hin und zurück?
tourist	Einfach.
clerk	Erster Klasse oder zweiter Klasse?
tourist	Zweiter Klasse, bitte.
clerk	50 Mark, bitte.
tourist	Wo muss ich umsteigen?
clerk	Sie müssen in Hannover umsteigen.

Übungen

1 Make phrases with the words. (*Answers on page 128.*)

1. eine | Hamburg | was | nach | Fahrkarte | kostet ?

2. aussteigen | muss | wo | ich ?

3. in | umsteigen | müssen | Hannover | Sie .

4. kaufe | Fahrkarten | wo | ich ?

5. am | Linie | 6 | Sie | besten | die | nehmen .

2 Listen to the two dialogues and make notes in English – you may not get the information to complete every box. (*Answers on page 128.*)

	1.	2.
where to?		
how (i.e. bus)?		
change – yes/no?		
what ticket?		
price?		

3 How would you say the phrases below? Practise them aloud. (*Answers on pages 128–9.*)

1. Which bus goes to the station?
2. Where do I get off?
3. Where do I buy tickets?
4. How much is a ticket to Berlin?
5. Do I have to change?

Tip

In this unit, you learned another form of the German word for 'I have to' (**ich muss**) – *Sie müssen* in Hannover umsteigen (you have to change in Hanover). Verbs like **müssen** are also known as modal verbs. They add more meaning to another verb in the sentence.

Modal verbs are used in almost the same way as in English: the second verb in the sentence takes the infinitive (the English 'to' … form of a verb), but in German it goes to the end of the sentence:

> Wo *muss* ich *umsteigen?*
> Wo *muss* ich *aussteigen?*
> Sie *müssen* am Martinsplatz *aussteigen*.
> Sie *müssen* am Bahnhof *umsteigen*.

Land und Leute

On German public transport you must 'cancel' your ticket in an **Entwerter** to make it valid, or you could face a large fine. These machines are usually clearly marked, but remember the handy phrase **Wo ist der Entwerter, bitte?** (Where is the cancelling machine, please?)

 # Accommodation

At the tourist office

Vokabular

ich rufe an	I('ll) call
dort ist alles voll	everything is full there
gibt es ein Hotel hier in der Nähe?	is there a hotel nearby?
soll ich ein Zimmer reservieren?	shall I book a room?
dort sind keine Zimmer frei?	there are no rooms vacant?
können Sie ein anderes Hotel empfehlen?	can you recommend another hotel?
eine Woche	one week
neben dem Bahnhof	next to the station
in der Gartenstraße	in Gartenstraße
Moment bitte	just a moment
gleich	just

 ### Dialog

assistant	Ja bitte? Kann ich Ihnen helfen?
tourist	Ja, gibt es ein Hotel hier in der Nähe?
assistant	Das Hotel Union ist gleich um die Ecke – neben dem Bahnhof. Soll ich ein Zimmer reservieren?
tourist	Ja bitte.
assistant	Ein Einzelzimmer oder ein Doppelzimmer?
tourist	Ein Einzelzimmer für eine Woche, bitte.
assistant	Mit Bad?
tourist	Nein, mit Dusche.
assistant	Moment bitte, ich rufe an. – Nein, dort ist alles voll.
tourist	Dort sind keine Zimmer frei?
assistant	Nein, leider nicht.
tourist	Können Sie ein anderes Hotel empfehlen?
assistant	Ja, die Pension Meyer in der Gartenstraße. Sie ist sehr schön und nicht zu teuer.
tourist	Vielen Dank!

Übungen

1   Match the questions on the left with the answers on the right. (*Answers on page 129.*)

1. Gibt es ein Hotel hier in der Nähe?   a) Nein, leider nicht.

2. Soll ich ein Zimmer reservieren?   b) Sie gehen um die Ecke rechts.

3. Dort sind keine Zimmer frei?   c) Ja bitte.

4. Wo ist das Hotel?   d) Ja, die Pension Meyer ist gleich um die Ecke.

2 Fill in the gaps with the words below. (*Answers on page 129.*)

1. Das _____ ist in der Gartenstraße.
2. Ich _____ an.
3. Ein Einzelzimmer für eine _____
4. Nein, dort ist alles _____ .
5. Können Sie ein anderes Hotel _____ ?
6. Die Pension Meyer ist _____ schön.

| Woche | sehr | rufe | voll | empfehlen | Hotel |

3 You can now use the phrases you have learned. You are at the tourist office and you are enquring about accommodation for yourself and your wife. Listen to the phrases on the recording and answer according to the notes below. (*Answers on page 129.*)

1. hotel or pension nearby?
2. yes – for my wife and me
3. double room with bathroom and TV
4. a week
5. no rooms vacant?
6. can you recommend another hotel?

Tip

In the previous unit you learned all about the modal verb 'to have to/must': **ich muss** (I have to/I must).

In this unit, you've learned a new modal verb – **sollen:** *Soll ich* **ein Zimmer reservieren?** (Shall I/Ought I to book a room?)

These are the other parts of **sollen** which you need to know:

Er/sie/es soll ein Zimmer reservieren.	He/she/it shall/ought to book a room.
Sie/sie sollen ein Zimmer reservieren.	You/they shall/ought to book a room.
Wir sollen ein Zimmer reservieren.	We shall/ought to book a room.

Land und Leute

Das Verkehrsamt (tourist information), also called **die Auskunft** or **das Informationsbüro**, is the place for information on accommodation, places of interest and public transport queries.

Hobbies and pastimes

Winter and summer

Dialog

Herr Braun	Haben Sie ein Hobby, Herr Meier?
Herr Meier	Ja, mein Hobby ist Sport. Ich fahre Ski.
Herr Braun	Und im Sommer? Was machen Sie im Sommer?
Herr Meier	Im Sommer spiele ich Tennis.
Herr Braun	Ja, ich finde Sport auch gut. Ich wandere, und ich schwimme jeden Tag.
Herr Meier	Und was machen Sie im Winter?
Herr Braun	Ich mache Skilanglauf. Das macht fit.
Herr Meier	Und Sie, Frau Klein? Machen Sie auch Sport?
Frau Klein	Ja, ich jogge jeden Tag.
Herr Braun	Auch im Winter?
Frau Klein	Nein, im Winter mache ich keinen Sport – im Winter ist es zu kalt!
Herr Braun	Haben Sie noch andere Hobbys?
Frau Klein	Ein anderes Hobby ist Malen. Aber am liebsten fotografiere ich.
Herr Braun	Und Sie, Herr Meier? Haben Sie noch andere Hobbys?
Herr Meier	Ja, ich koche sehr gern. Und ich spiele gern Schach.
Herr Braun	Mein anderes Hobby ist Kino. Ich mag Filme – ich gehe jedes Wochenende ins Kino.

Übungen

1   Make sentences with the words. (*Answers on page 129.*)

1. `fahre` `Winter` `ich` `Ski` `im` .

2. `liebsten` `schwimme` `am` `ich` .

3. jeden │ ich │ jogge │ Tag .

4. Hobby │ Schach │ mein │ ist │ anderes .

5. Tennis │ spiele │ ich │ Sommer │ im .

6. Wochenende │ koche │ ich │ jedes .

2 Listen to the dialogue and read the sentences below. Are they true or false? (*Answers on page 129.*)

	true	false
1. In the summer he goes hiking.	☐	☐
2. In the winter she does cross-country skiing.	☐	☐
3. His favourite hobby is cooking.	☐	☐
4. Her other hobby is sports.	☐	☐
5. He plays tennis every day.	☐	☐

3 Now it's your turn to talk about hobbies. Listen to the phrases on the recording and respond in the pauses, using the information below. (*Answers on page 129.*)

1. yes – your hobby: sports
2. summer: tennis + you jog every day
3. winter: cross-country skiing
4. you like chess – but cooking best
5. what do you do in the winter?
6. you too like books

Tip

Remember from Unit 12 that the verb follows directly an expression of time at the beginning of a sentence?

Im Sommer *spiele* ich Tennis.   **Im Winter *mache* ich keinen Sport.**

If you want to look up a German verb in a dictionary, you have to know its infinitive (the English 'to …' form of a verb). German infinitives always end in **-n** or **-en**: **nehmen** (to take), **regnen** (to rain).

Land und Leute

Football is the most popular sport in Germany. Other popular sports are swimming, cycling and tennis. In Germany, too, people like to try out new types of sports. Mountain-biking and roller-blading are very popular – not only among the younger generation.

Towns and villages

Sightseeing

Vokabular

sieht man ...?	does one see ...?
besichtigen	to visit/to have a look at
einen Spaziergang machen	to go for a stroll
ich gebe Ihnen	I'll give you
eine Stadtrundfahrt	a sightseeing tour
eine Broschüre	a brochure
über Münster	about/on Münster
durch die Innenstadt	through the centre of town
der Dom	the cathedral
eine Liste von	a list of
einen Stadtplan	a map
berühmt	famous

Dialog

assistant	Guten Tag! Kann ich Ihnen helfen?
tourist	Guten Tag. Ich bin für zwei Tage in Münster. Ich möchte die Stadt besichtigen.
assistant	Münster ist eine schöne alte Stadt. Hier gibt es viel zu sehen!
tourist	Was können Sie empfehlen? Eine Stadtrundfahrt?
assistant	Ja, die Stadtrundfahrt ist sehr interessant.
tourist	Sieht man viele Sehenswürdigkeiten?
assistant	Ja, sehr viele. Sie können auch einen Spaziergang machen – durch die Innenstadt. Der Dom und die alten Kirchen sind sehr berühmt.
tourist	Danke.
assistant	Hier – ich gebe Ihnen eine Broschüre über Münster.
tourist	Vielen Dank. Haben Sie auch eine Liste von Hotels und Restaurants?
assistant	Ja, hier – bitte.
tourist	Ich möchte auch einen Stadtplan, bitte.
assistant	Bitte sehr!

Übungen

1 Match the parts of words on the left with the ones on the right. (*Answers on page 129.*)

1. STADT	a) GANG
2. SEHENS	b) RUNDFAHRT
3. INNEN	c) WÜRDIGKEITEN
4. SPAZIER	d) PLAN
5. STADT	e) STADT

2   Listen to the dialogue and fill in the answers in English. (*Answers on page 129.*)

town	assistant recommends	customer asks for

3   Now it's your turn to go to the tourist office. Listen to what the assistant is saying on the recording and respond using the notes below. (*Answers on page 129.*)

1. yes – you'd like to visit the town
2. can you recommed a sightseeing tour?
3. do you see many sights?
4. brochure of Berlin?
5. a list of hotels and restaurants?
6. you'd also like a map, please

Tip

In Unit 9, you learned that articles can change their endings according to the noun they go with. The changes depend on the gender of the noun (**der, die, das**) and how the noun functions in the sentence:

Hier ist ein Stadtplan. →	**Sie haben ein*en* Stadtplan.**
Stadtplan is the subject.	**Sie** is the subject. **Stadtplan** is the object.
der Stadtplan (subject)	**Sie haben de*n* Stadtplan**. (object)

The masculine article **ein (der)** changes to **ein*en* (de*n*)** when its noun is the object of the sentence – it has something done to it. The articles for feminine, neuter and plural nouns stay the same:

Hier ist eine (die) Broschüre. (subject)	**Sie haben eine (die) Broschüre.** (object)
Hier ist ein (das) Hemd. (subject)	**Sie haben ein (das) Hemd**. (object)

Land und Leute

The German word for postcard is **die Ansichtskarte** (plural **Ansichtskarten**). You can buy stamps (**Briefmarken**) at the post office or at newsagents or tobacconists. German post boxes (**ein Briefkasten**) are yellow.

Vokabular

sagen Sie	tell me
wir wollen einen Ausflug machen	we want to go on an excursion
wir verreisen	we're going on holiday
nach Griechenland	to Greece
zum Skifahren	skiing
nach Kalifornien	to California
im Frühling	in the spring
im Herbst	in the autumn
zu Ostern	at Easter
in den Sommerferien	in the summer break
dieses Jahr	this year
für zwei Wochen	for two weeks
stimmt	(that's) true

Dialog

Herr Schmidt	Sagen Sie, was machen Sie zu Ostern, Frau Klein?
Frau Klein	Wir wollen einen Ausflug machen. Aber das Wetter ist zu schlecht!
Herr Schmidt	Ja, stimmt – im Frühling ist es oft sehr kalt. Und was machen Sie im Sommer?
Frau Klein	Wir verreisen. Wir fahren nach Griechenland. Was machen Sie in den Sommerferien, Herr Schmidt?
Herr Schmidt	Also, wir verreisen dieses Jahr im Herbst.
Frau Klein	Und wohin fahren Sie?
Herr Schmidt	Wir fahren für zwei Wochen nach Amerika – nach Kalifornien.
Frau Klein	Oh, schön! Und Sie, Herr Braun? Verreisen Sie dieses Jahr?
Herr Braun	Ja, ich fahre im Winter zum Skifahren – nach Österreich.
Frau Klein	Nach Österreich – wie interessant! Fahren Sie im Januar oder im Februar?
Herr Braun	Nein, ich fahre im Dezember – dann ist es noch nicht zu kalt.

Übungen

1 Look at the ads and put the right number by the statements opposite. (*Answers on page 129.*)

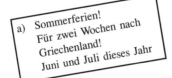

a) Sommerferien!
   Für zwei Wochen nach Griechenland!
   Juni und Juli dieses Jahr

b) Im Winter nach Amerika
   – zum Skifahren!
   Eine Woche
   (November/Dezember)

c) Drei Tage Berlin
   Machen Sie einen
   Ausflug zu Ostern!
   Mit Stadtrundfahrt!

1. You only have one week – which holiday is for you?
2. You fancy a city break.
3. You want a sunny holiday.
4. You can only go in November or December.
5. You want to go away over Easter.
6. You have to go in June or July.

2 Now it's your turn to ask about holiday plans. Say the English questions below in German. (*Answers on page 129.*)

1. what are you doing in autumn?
2. ... in spring?
3. ... in the summer break?
4. ... for Easter?
5. ... in winter?

3 Listen to the different months on the recording and say the month that follows in the pause. You will hear an example first. (*Answers on page 129.*)

Tip

In some of the previous units, you learned where expressions of time (**am Sonntag, im Winter, jeden Tag**) can go in a sentence. But sometimes more information is added to a sentence: not only *when* (time) you are doing something, but also *how* (manner) and *where* (place). Where do all this elements go in a sentence? The rule is easy:

time	manner	place

Ich fahre – im Winter – mit dem Zug – nach Österreich.

Land und Leute

German employees have amongst the highest number of holidays in Europe. It is quite common to have up to 31 days paid leave per year, and on top of that there are the bank holidays (**Feiertage**) which are also free!

Extravokabular

im Januar	(in) January
Februar	February
März	March
April	April
Mai	May
Juni	June
Juli	July
August	August
September	September
Oktober	October
November	November
Dezember	December

Problems

'I've lost something!'

Vokabular

ich habe meine Tasche verloren	I've lost my bag
Sie haben Ihre Tasche verloren?	you've lost your bag?
haben Sie eine Tasche gefunden?	have you found a bag?
was war drin?	what was in it?
das Fundbüro	the lost property office
die Polizei	the police
meine Geldbörse	my wallet
mein Pass	my passport
meine Kamera	my camera
meine Schlüssel	my keys
Ihre Adresse	your address
beim Einkaufen	while out shopping
null	zero

Dialoge

Julia Braun	Entschuldigung! Ich habe meine Tasche verloren. Wo ist das Fundbüro?
passer-by	Sie haben Ihre Tasche verloren? Sie gehen am besten zur Polizei.
Julia Braun	Wo finde ich die Polizei, bitte?
passer-by	Gehen Sie um die Ecke und dann die dritte Straße links. Dort ist die Polizei.
Julia Braun	Danke.

Julia Braun	Guten Tag!
policeman	Guten Tag! Ja?
Julia Braun	Ich habe meine Tasche verloren!
policeman	Wo haben Sie Ihre Tasche verloren?
Julia Braun	In der Stadt – beim Einkaufen. Haben Sie eine Tasche gefunden?
policeman	Einen Moment bitte. – Nein, leider nicht. Was war drin?
Julia Braun	Mein Pass, meine Kamera und meine Geldbörse – und meine Schlüssel.
policeman	Also – Ihr Name und Ihre Adresse, bitte?
Julia Braun	Mein Name ist Julia Braun. Meine Adresse ist Goldstraße 25, 10575 Berlin.

Übungen

 1 Listen to the three people in the lost property office. Write down the details for each person in English. (*Answers on page 129.*)

1. lost what?	2. lost what (colour)?	3. lost what?
contents?	contents?	where?

2   Match the German ads on the left with the illustrations on the right. (*Answers on page 129.*)

1.
| Verloren! |
| Eine braune Tasche |
| Telefon 60 20 31 |

a)

2.
| Gefunden im Park! |
| Geldbörse (schwarz) |
| Telefon 60 98 901 |

b)

3.
| Verloren: |
| eine Kamera (neu) |
| Frau Schmidt |
| Gartenstraße 23 |

c)

4.
| Gefunden |
| Pass (deutsch) |
| Thomas Klose |
| Telefon 66 73 93 |

d)

3   Now you have lost something. You will be asked what you've lost. Look at the prompts below. Each time, repeat the missing items in the pause, adding a new one at the end. (*Answers on page 129.*)

1.   2.   3.   4.   5.

Tip

You know already how to use verbs in the present tense. Sometimes you will have to use the past tense, though – when you want to describe something that happened in the past. The past tense is usually formed with the verb **haben** (to have). As in English, when using the past tense with **haben**, the second verb changes its form, but in German the second part also goes to the end of the sentence:

| **Sie *finden* eine Tasche.** | **Sie *haben* eine Tasche *gefunden*.** |
| You find a bag. | You have found a bag. |

For the moment, try to learn and practise the whole phrase rather than learning all the words separately!

Land und Leute

Having your property stolen when abroad can be distressing. Make sure you have travel insurance and ask at the **Rezeption** of your hotel whether you can keep your valuables in the safe.

UNIT 36 The present, the future and the past

Jobs

Dialog

Herr Braun	Seit wann wohnen Sie in Berlin, Frau Klein?
Frau Klein	Ich wohne seit drei Jahren in Berlin.
Herr Braun	Wo haben Sie früher gewohnt?
Frau Klein	Früher habe ich in Bonn gewohnt.
Herr Braun	Was haben Sie in Bonn gemacht?
Frau Klein	Ich habe dort in einer Bank gearbeitet.
Herr Braun	Und was machen Sie jetzt?
Frau Klein	Ich bin Sekretärin. Und Sie, Herr Braun? Seit wann wohnen Sie in Berlin?
Herr Braun	Seit Ostern.
Frau Klein	Und wo haben Sie früher gewohnt?
Herr Braun	Früher habe ich in München gewohnt.
Frau Klein	Was haben Sie dort gemacht?
Herr Braun	Ich war Verkäufer. Ich habe Autos verkauft.
Frau Klein	Und was machen Sie jetzt?
Herr Braun	Ich arbeite in einem Kaufhaus. Ich verkaufe Bücher.

Übungen

1 Match the questions with the answers opposite. (*Answers on page 129.*)

1. Wo haben Sie früher gewohnt?
2. Was machen Sie jetzt?
3. Seit wann wohnen Sie in Hamburg?
4. Was haben Sie dort gemacht?

a) Ich habe Autos verkauft.
b) Seit sechs Jahren.
c) Ich bin Sekretärin.
d) In München.

2   Listen to the dialogue and fill in the details in English. (*Answers on page 129.*)

lives where?		for how long?	
used to live in?		used to be?	
is now?		husband?	

3   Listen to the phrases and respond in the pauses on the recording using the English prompts below. (*Answers on the recording and on page 129.*)

1. I've lived in Berlin for four years.
2. I used to live in Hamburg.
3. I've lived in Berlin for two years.
4. I was in a hotel there.

Tip

Note that, when stating your job, you say the equivalent of 'I am sales assistant' or 'I am secretary' – you do not use the word for 'a':

Ich bin Sekretärin.   **Ich bin Verkäufer.**

Land und Leute

Some 70 per cent of all Germans between the age of 16 and 65 are in regular employment. About 3.7 million people in Germany are unemployed; the rate in the West is around 8%, in the East it is higher, around 15%. German wages are amongst the highest in Europe – the average gross salary per year is 36 000 DM. Almost all German employees receive a '13th monthly wage' at Christmas and a lot of Germans rely on this **Weihnachtsgeld** (Christmas money) to pay for all the Christmas presents!

Self and others

'What does he look like?'

Vokabular

haben Sie Sandra gesehen?	have you seen Sandra?
wie sieht sie denn aus?	what does she look like?
Herrn Kunze kenne ich nicht	I don't know Mr Kunze
Herrn Kunze habe ich nicht gesehen	I haven't seen Mr Kunze
er trägt eine Brille	he wears glasses
groß	tall
schlank	slim
dick	fat
blaue/grüne Augen	blue/green eyes
einen braunen Schnurrbart	a brown moustache
schwarze lockige Haare	black curly hair
kurze/lange blonde Haare	short/long blond hair
eine Glatze	a bald head

Dialoge

Frau Braun Sandra! Sandra! Oh, Herr Müller, haben Sie Sandra gesehen?

Herr Müller Sandra ist Ihre kleine Tochter, nicht wahr? Wie sieht sie denn aus?

Frau Braun Sie ist klein und ziemlich dick. Sie hat blaue Augen und blonde Haare.

Herr Müller Hat sie kurze blonde Haare?

Frau Braun Nein, sie hat lange blonde Haare ... Ach, da ist sie ja! Sandra! Sandra!!

Herr Braun Herr Müller, haben Sie Herrn Kunze gesehen?

Herr Müller Tag, Herr Braun. Herrn Kunze? Nein, Herrn Kunze kenne ich nicht. Wie sieht er denn aus?

Herr Braun Also, er ist groß und schlank. Er hat grüne Augen, und er trägt eine Brille.

Herr Müller Ach ja ... hat er schwarze lockige Haare?

Herr Braun Nein, er hat eine Glatze – und einen braunen Schnurrbart.

Herr Müller Nein, es tut mir leid – Herrn Kunze habe ich nicht gesehen.

Übungen

1 Match each illustration with the right phrase. (*Answers on page 129.*)

1.
   a) Sie ist groß und dick.
   b) Sie ist klein und schlank.

2.
   a) Er hat blonde lockige Haare.
   b) Er hat eine Glatze.

3. a) Ich trage eine Brille.
b) Ich habe einen Schnurrbart.

4. a) Er hat kurze lockige Haare.
b) Er hat lange lockige Haare.

2 Listen to the dialogues at the police station and fill in the policeman's form in English. (*Answers on page 129.*)

	name	sex	age	description
1.				
2.				

3 Now it's your turn to speak. Answer the questions on the recording according to the notes below. (*Answers on page 129.*)

1. blue eyes
2. bald
3. short and fat

Tip

In this unit you learned how to describe what other people look like. When describing yourself/someone else, you need to use the irregular verbs **sein** (to be) and **haben** (to have). You have already come across the forms for **sein** in Unit 5 and for **haben** in Unit 11.

tragen (to wear) is another irregular verb. You can look up its other forms in Unit 26 – they are the same as for the verb **fahren**.

Land und Leute

By no means all German people correspond to the stereotype of the tall, blue-eyed blonde – like other nationalities, they come in all shapes and sizes! German people like to dress fashionably, and you'll see many small children sporting very colourful outfits.

Food and drink

Snacks

Vokabular

was darf's sein?	what would you like?
eine Bockwurst	a cooked sausage
eine Frikadelle	a meatball
ein halbes Hähnchen	half a grilled chicken
eine Currywurst	a fried sausage with curry sauce
Salat	salad
Senf	mustard
Ketschup	tomato sauce
Majonäse	mayonnaise
eine Cola	a coke
einen Orangensaft	an orange juice

Dialoge

vendor	Guten Tag! Was darf's sein?
customer	Ich möchte eine Bratwurst, bitte.
vendor	Gern. Mit Ketschup oder mit Majonäse?
customer	Nein, mit Senf und mit Pommes frites, bitte.
vendor	Also: eine Bratwurst mit Senf und Pommes frites.
customer	Und eine Frikadelle mit Salat, bitte.
vendor	Und mit Pommes frites?
customer	Nein, ohne Pommes frites. Und mein Mann möchte eine Bockwurst.
vendor	Eine große oder eine kleine Bockwurst?
customer	Eine große Bockwurst, bitte. Und eine Cola und einen Orangensaft.
vendor	Kommt sofort!
vendor	Ja bitte?
customer 2	Ein halbes Hähnchen, bitte.
vendor	Es tut mir leid – Hähnchen haben wir heute nicht.
customer 2	Dann nehme ich eine Currywurst mit Pommes frites und mit Ketschup und Majonäse.
vendor	Eine Currywurst mit Pommes frites und mit Ketschup und Majonäse – bitte sehr.

Übungen

1   Find the right response for each phrase. (*Answers on page 129.*)

1. Eine Bratwurst, bitte!

   a) Eine große Cola?
   b) Mit Senf oder Ketschup?

2. Ich möchte ein halbes Hähnchen und eine Cola, bitte!

   a) Eine Bratwurst mit Senf.
   b) Mit Kartoffelsalat?

3. Eine Bockwurst mit Pommes frites, bitte.

   a) Möchten Sie Ketschup?
   b) Eine Bratwurst mit Pommes.

4. Ich möchte einen Orangensaft und eine Frikadelle, bitte.

   a) Möchten Sie Salat?
   b) Eine große Cola.

5. Eine Currywurst und Salat!

   a) Eine Currywurst mit Ketschup.
   b) Und zu trinken?

6. Was darf's sein?

   a) Eine Bockwurst mit Salat, bitte.
   b) Mit Ketschup oder mit Majonäse?

2 Listen to the dialogue and fill in the details in English. (*Answers on page 129.*)

	to eat	with	to drink
customer 1			
customer 2			

3 You are ordering snacks for your family. Respond to the questions on the recording according to the notes below. (*Answers on the recording and on page 129.*)

1. fried sausage with mustard
2. cooked sausage with salad
3. small cooked sausage
4. meatball with fries and tomato sauce
5. a large coke and an orange juice

Tip

To ask for two or more meals, use **zweimal, dreimal** etc.:

Zweimal Currywurst mit Pommes frites, bitte!

Land und Leute

Germany has many different types of fast food outlets (**die Imbissbude**). Very popular are chips with mayonnaise and ketchup – quite often both together! This is called **Pommes rot-weiß** (chips red-white), with **Pommes** pronounced as 'Thomas' with a P. Turkish fast food stalls or shops are also very popular in Germany due to the large number of Turkish foreign workers who introduced their cuisine to the country in the 1960s and 70s. The dish to try there is **Gyros Pitta** or **Gyros Rollo** – a pitta bread filled with shredded spit-roasted beef, onions and latherings of creamy garlic sauce.

Shopping

Different types of food

Vokabular

wo kaufe ich am besten Lebensmittel?	where's the best place to buy groceries?
was brauchen Sie denn?	what do you need?
ich bin zu Besuch hier	I'm just visiting here
ich muß einkaufen	I have to go shopping
ich brauche Tomaten	I need tomatoes
Aufschnitt kaufen Sie in der Metzgerei	you can buy cold meats at the butcher's
in der Gemüsehandlung	at the greengrocer's
Brot kaufe ich immer in der Bäckerei	I always buy bread at the bakery

Dialog

tourist	Entschuldigung.
passer-by	Kann ich Ihnen helfen?
tourist	Ich bin zu Besuch hier – ich muss einkaufen. Aber wo kaufe ich am besten Lebensmittel?
passer-by	Ja, was brauchen Sie denn?
tourist	Also, ich brauche Wurst, Aufschnitt, Tomaten, Brot ...
passer-by	Wurst und Aufschnitt kaufen Sie in der Metzgerei um die Ecke.
tourist	Und Tomaten – wo kaufe ich am besten Tomaten?
passer-by	In der Gemüsehandlung am Marktplatz. Und Brot – Brot kaufe ich immer in der Bäckerei in der Gartenstraße.
tourist	Ach ja – die Bäckerei in der Gartenstraße ...
passer-by	Sonst noch etwas?
tourist	Nein, das ist alles. Vielen Dank.

Übungen

1 Match the phrases with the right shop signs. (*Answers on page 129.*)

1. Ich brauche Aufschnitt.   a) **Metzgerei** b) (**Post**)

2. Wo kaufe ich am besten Tomaten?   a) (Bahnhof)   b) ◁ Gemüsehandlung ▷

3. Ich brauche auch Brot.   a) ⟨ Bäckerei ⟩   b) **Bank**

4. Wo kaufe ich Wurst?   a) **Restaurant**   b) (*Metzgerei*)

2 Listen to the dialogue. Are the statements true or false? (*Answers on page 129.*)

	true	false
1. Herr Sauer buys bread at the bakery at the station.	☐	☐
2. Herr Meier is buying vegetables and cold meats.	☐	☐
3. He buys vegetables at the same place as Herr Sauer.	☐	☐
4. He recommends a butcher's shop to Herr Sauer.	☐	☐

3 Your best friend is asking ridiculous questions about where to buy goods. Correct him in the pauses using the information below. (*Answers on page 129.*)

1.   2.  3.   4.

Tip

Do you remember when to use the polite (formal) form of 'you', **Sie**, and when to use the informal **du**? Let's recap: **du** is only used for children, members of families, close friends and animals – for everybody else (and when in doubt) use **Sie**.

Land und Leute

Other German words for shops:

book store	**die Buchhandlung**
stationer's	**die Schreibwarenhandlung**
ladies' fashion shop	**die Damenmoden**
men's fashion shop	**die Herrenmoden/der Herrenausstatter**
shoe shop	**die Schuhhandlung/das Schuhhaus**

Directions

'Where's the post office?'

Vokabular

hallo!	hello!/excuse me!
die Telefonzelle	the phone box
durch den Fußgängertunnel	through the pedestrian subway
an der Ampel	at the traffic lights
die Brücke	the bridge
der Supermarkt	the supermarket
Briefmarken	stamps
meine Postkarten	my postcards
hier um die Ecke	around the corner here
über	over/above
hinter	behind
vor	in front of

Dialog

tourist	Hallo! Hallo!
passer-by	Ja?
tourist	Wo ist die nächste Telefonzelle, bitte?
passer-by	Die nächste Telefonzelle? Also – Sie gehen hier um die Ecke.
tourist	Hier um die Ecke ...
passer-by	Ja. Gehen Sie links durch den Fußgängertunnel. Gehen Sie dann über die Brücke.
tourist	Über die Brücke – ja.
passer-by	Dort ist der Supermarkt. Die Telefonzelle ist vor dem Supermarkt.
tourist	Vor dem Supermarkt – vielen Dank. Ach ja – und ich brauche Briefmarken für meine Postkarten. Wo ist die nächste Post, bitte?
passer-by	Gehen Sie an der Ampel links – bis zur Apotheke. Die Post ist gleich hinter der Apotheke.
tourist	Vielen Dank.

Übungen

1 Match each phrase with the right response. (*Answers on page 129.*)

1. Ich brauche Briefmarken.
2. Vielen Dank.
3. Wo ist die nächste Telefonzelle?
4. Ich brauche Brot und Äpfel.

a) Der Supermarkt ist gleich um die Ecke.
b) Sie gehen über die Brücke und dann rechts.
c) Die Post ist neben der Apotheke.
d) Gern geschehen!

2 Listen to the dialogue and answer the questions below in English.
(*Answers on pages 129–30.*)

1. What is the man looking for?
2. What directions is he given?
3. What does the woman say about the nearest telephone box?

3 Now it's your turn to give directions in the pauses on the recording. You will be
asked where various places are. Reply according to the pictures below.
(*Answers on the recording and on page 130.*)

1. Bank

2. Apotheke

3. Telefonzelle

4. Supermarkt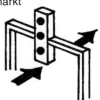

Tip

Here are more rules for prepositions:

For **durch** and **um**:		
der Fußgängertunnel	→	**durch** *den* Fußgängertunnel
die Stadt	→	**durch die** Stadt
das Haus	→	**durch das** Haus

For **zu**:		
der Fußgängertunnel	→	*zu dem/zum* Fußgängertunnel
die Stadt	→	*zu der/zur* Stadt
das Haus	→	*zu dem/zum* Haus

an, **über**, **hinter**, **vor**, **in**, **auf** and **neben** take either of those endings. If they
indicate a movement (i.e. used with verbs like **gehen**, 'to go'), they follow the rules
for **durch**. If used with verbs like **wohnen** (to live), they follow the rules for **zu**.

Land und Leute

Hallo! (hello!) is a useful informal greeting. But **hallo!** can have another meaning
too: in the dialogue in this unit, the tourist used **Hallo! Hallo!** to attract the
passer-by's attention.

Numbers

Money: Numbers over 100

Vokabular

einen Scheck einlösen	to cash a cheque
für 250 Pfund D-Mark	£250 into D-Mark
300 Pfund in Schweizer Franken wechseln	to change £300 into Swiss Francs
Dollar in D-Mark wechseln	to change $ into D-Mark
unterschreiben Sie hier bitte	sign here please
wieviel Geld möchten Sie?	how much money would you like?
kann ich damit Geld abheben?	can I withdraw money with it?
einen Reisescheck	a traveller's cheque
Ihren Ausweis	your identification
eine Frage	a question
eine Euroscheckkarte	a eurocheque card

Dialog

tourist Guten Tag, ich möchte einen Scheck einlösen.

clerk Ja, gern – einen Euroscheck oder einen Reisescheck?

tourist Einen Reisescheck.

clerk Und wieviel Geld möchten Sie?

tourist Ich möchte für 250 Pfund D-Mark.

clerk Gern. Ihren Ausweis, bitte.

tourist Hier – mein Ausweis.

clerk Danke. So, 250 Pfund in D-Mark – das sind 576 Mark. Unterschreiben Sie hier bitte.

tourist Hier, bitte. Und ich möchte 300 Pfund in Schweizer Franken wechseln.

clerk 300 Pfund in Schweizer Franken – das sind 539 Franken.

tourist Danke. Ich möchte auch Dollar in D-Mark wechseln. Und ich habe noch eine Frage: Ich habe eine Euroscheckkarte. Kann ich damit Geld abheben?

clerk Ja, Sie können damit Geld vom Geldautomaten abheben.

Übungen

1 Match the German and English phrases. (*Answers on page 130.*)

1. Ich möchte für 200 Pfund D-Mark.
   a) I would like German marks for £200.
   b) I would like 200 German marks.

2. Unterschreiben Sie hier bitte.
   a) Can I see your passport, please.
   b) Please sign here.

3. Kann ich damit Geld abheben?
   a) Can I change some money, please?
   b) Can I withdraw money with that?

4. Ich möchte einen Scheck einlösen.
   a) I want to cash a cheque.
   b) Please sign here.

5. Ich möchte 300 Pfund wechseln.
   a) I'd like to change 300 pounds.
   b) I'd like to withdraw 300 pounds.

2 Listen to the dialogue in the bank and write down the numbers as you hear them. (*Answers on page 130.*)

£
DM

£
FR

3 Now it's your turn to change money. Listen to the bank clerk's questions and respond using the information below. (*Answers on the recording and on page 130.*)

1. you want to cash a traveller's cheque
2. £200 into DM
3. you'd like to change £150 into Swiss francs
4. change $250 into DM
5. and change $300 into Swiss francs

Tip

Do you remember how to form numbers above 100?

100 + 1	= **einhundert(und)eins**	= 101
200 + 20	= **zweihundert(und)zwanzig**	= 220
300 + 4 + 30	= **dreihundert(und)vierunddreißig**	= 334

All other numbers up to 999 are formed the same way.

Land und Leute

You can change money in Germany at a bank (**die Bank**), a building society (**die Sparkasse**) or an exchange bureau (**die Wechselstube**). As in other countries, all these places will charge you a small amount for changing your money. It is a good idea to get a conversion chart before you come to Germany so you know at a glance how much things cost roughly.

Public transport

Travelling to work

Vokabular

was sind Sie von Beruf?	what's your profession?
wo arbeiten Sie?	where do you work?
wie fahren Sie zur Arbeit?	how do you travel to work?
wie lange dauert denn die Fahrt?	so how long is the journey?
Architekt	architect
Ärztin	doctor (female)
Ihr Büro	your office
in der Innenstadt	in the centre of town
im Krankenhaus	at the hospital
mit dem Auto	by car
mit dem Fahrrad	by bicycle
ich meine	I mean
ach so	I see

Dialog

Frau Klein	Sagen Sie – was sind Sie von Beruf, Herr Müller?
Herr Müller	Ich? Ich bin Architekt von Beruf.
Frau Klein	Und wo arbeiten Sie? Ich meine: Wo ist Ihr Büro?
Herr Müller	Mein Büro ist in der Innenstadt, in der Marktstraße.
Frau Klein	Wie fahren Sie zur Arbeit, Herr Müller? Mit dem Auto?
Herr Müller	Nein, ich fahre mit dem Bus zur Arbeit.
Frau Klein	Ach so, mit dem Bus. Wie lange dauert denn die Fahrt?
Herr Müller	Also, die Fahrt dauert 45 Minuten.
Frau Klein	Müssen Sie auch umsteigen?
Herr Müller	Ja, ich muss am Schillerplatz umsteigen. Und Sie, Frau Klein? Was sind Sie von Beruf?
Frau Klein	Ich bin Ärztin von Beruf. Ich arbeite im Krankenhaus neben dem Bahnhof.
Herr Müller	Und wie fahren Sie zur Arbeit? Mit dem Bus oder mit dem Auto?
Frau Klein	Nein, im Sommer fahre ich mit dem Fahrrad, und im Winter fahre ich mit der U-Bahn.

Übungen

1 Match each illustration with the right phrase. (*Answers on page 130.*)

1.
   a) Ich bin Architekt von Beruf.
   b) Ich bin Ärztin von Beruf.

2.
   a) Wie fahren Sie zur Arbeit?
   b) Wie lange dauert die Fahrt?

3.   a) Ich fahre mit dem Bus zur Arbeit.
   b) Ich fahre mit dem Auto zur Arbeit.

4.   a) Wo arbeiten Sie?
   b) Was sind Sie von Beruf?

2 Listen to the monologue and make notes in English for the following. (*Answers on page 130.*)

name	age
lives in	job
works in	travels to work by
hobbies	

3 Respond to the questions using the information below. (*Answers on page 130.*)

1. architect
2. you work in the centre of town
3. no – you travel to work by bus
4. journey takes 30 minutes

Tip

Do you remember how questions are formed?

Wie	**fahren**	**Sie zur Arbeit?**
question word	verb	rest of the sentence

Here is a list of all the question words you have learned so far:

wie?	how?	**wo?**	where?	**was?**	what?
wann?	when?	**welche/r/s?**	which?	**wieviel?**	how much?
woher?	where from?	**wohin?**	where to?	**wie lange?**	how long?
seit wann?	since when?/for how long?				

Land und Leute

The Germans and the Swiss are very environmentally-conscious. In Germany new cars have to be fitted with a catalytic converter and there are strict emission tests. Car-sharing to and from work is quite common.

Accommodation

Booking into a hotel

Vokabular

ich habe ein Zimmer reserviert	I've booked a room
wann gibt es Frühstück?	when is breakfast being served?
mit Balkon	with balcony
mit Telefon	with telephone
mit Blick auf die Berge	with a view of the mountains
Ihr Anmeldeformular	your registration form
Ihr Schlüssel	your key
der Speiseraum	the dining room
das Abendessen	dinner
der Parkplatz	the car park

Dialog

Herr Meier Guten Tag. Ich habe ein Zimmer reserviert.
receptionist Ihr Name bitte?
Herr Meier Peter Meier.
receptionist Ja, Herr Meier – ein Einzelzimmer mit Balkon und mit Telefon. Hier ist Ihr Anmeldeformular.
Herr Meier Danke.
receptionist So, Zimmer neunzehn – Ihr Zimmer ist im ersten Stock. Hier ist Ihr Schlüssel.
Herr Meier Vielen Dank. Ist das Zimmer ruhig?
receptionist Ja, das Zimmer ist sehr schön und ruhig. Es ist mit Blick auf die Berge.
Herr Meier Danke. Wo ist der Speiseraum, bitte?
receptionist Der Speiseraum ist im Untergeschoss.
Herr Meier Und wann gibt es Frühstück und Abendessen?
receptionist Frühstück gibt es von 7 bis 9 Uhr. Abendessen gibt es von 19 bis 22 Uhr.
Herr Meier Danke. Und wo ist der Parkplatz?
receptionist Der Parkplatz ist gleich um die Ecke, hinter dem Garten.
Herr Meier Vielen Dank. Wo ist der Fahrstuhl, bitte?
receptionist Dort drüben rechts.

Übungen

1 Match the words or phrases with the right illustration. (*Answers on page 130.*)

1. der Speiseraum   a)    b)

2. Ihr Schlüssel   a)   b)

3. der Parkplatz   a)   b)

4. ein Zimmer mit Aussicht auf die Berge   a)   b)

5. Ihr Anmeldeformular   a)   b)

2 Listen to the dialogue and connect the items mentioned with the correct floor. (*Answers on page 130.*)

3 You are booking into a hotel with your family. Listen to what the receptionist says and answer accordingly, using the notes below. (*Answers on the recording and on page 130.*)

1. you booked two rooms
2. no – double room for you/wife + single for daughter
3. no – with balcony and phone
4. are they with view of mountains?
5. full board – dining room?
6. breakfast and dinner – when?

Tip

reserviert is the past participle of **reservieren**, just like **gemacht** or **gearbeitet**. But with verbs ending in **-ieren** you do not need to add **ge-** when you form the past participle. Similarly **telefonieren – ich habe telefoniert**.

Land und Leute

When staying in hotels in German-speaking countries, you might come across a number of signs on doors, in rooms or outside. If you want to know where the entrance or exit is, look out for **der Eingang** and **der Ausgang** (for people) or **die Einfahrt** and **die Ausfahrt** (for cars).

Hobbies and pastimes

'But what about the weather?'

Vokabular

wie geht es dir?	how are you? (*informal*)
wollen wir uns treffen?	shall we meet?
morgen soll es Regen geben	it's supposed to rain tomorrow
übermorgen	the day after tomorrow
ein Gewitter	a thunderstorm
es soll windig sein	it's supposed to be windy
ich zeige dir	I'll show you
im Park	in the park

Dialog

Ute Kaiser	Kaiser!
Thomas Schmidt	Hallo, Ute! Wie geht es dir?
Ute Kaiser	Hallo, Thomas ...
Thomas Schmidt	Du, Ute, wollen wir uns diese Woche treffen? Hast du Zeit?
Ute Kaiser	Also – ich weiß nicht ...
Thomas Schmidt	Wie wäre es mit morgen? Im Park gibt es ein Konzert!
Ute Kaiser	Nein, nein, das Wetter ist zu schlecht. Morgen soll es Regen geben.
Thomas Schmidt	Ja, das stimmt. Wie wäre es mit übermorgen? Ich zeige dir die Stadt.
Ute Kaiser	Nein, übermorgen soll es ein Gewitter geben.
Thomas Schmidt	Und wie wäre es mit Donnerstag? Donnerstag soll es sonnig sein.
Ute Kaiser	Ähh, nein – Donnerstag soll es zu heiß sein – und es soll windig sein.
Thomas Schmidt	Ja, und Freitag?
Ute Kaiser	Nein, Freitag soll es schneien.
Thomas Schmidt	Ich weiß – wie wäre es mit Sonnabend?
Ute Kaiser	Ähh ...

Übungen

1 Make phrases with the words below. (*Answers on page 130.*)

1. es | Freitag | schneien | soll .

2. Regen | soll | geben | morgen | es .

3. übermorgen | sonnig | soll | es | sein .

4. soll | ein | Gewitter | es | geben | Montag .

5. morgen | es | sein | soll | windig .

6. zu | Donnerstag | sein | heiß | es | soll .

Cross reference with units:

2 Listen to the dialogue and answer the questions in English. (*Answers on page 130.*)

1. Why are they not meeting tomorrow?
2. What's the weather supposed to be like the day after tomorrow?
3. What day are they arranging to meet?
4. What are they arranging to do when they meet?

3 Now it's your turn to talk about the weather. Listen to the questions on the recording and respond in the pauses with the information below. (*Answers on the recording and on page 130.*)

1.

Tomorrow: no

2.

The day after tomorrow: no

3.

Monday: no

4.

Wednesday: no

5.

Thursday: no

6.

Friday: yes

Tip

In this unit, you learned another modal verb: *Wollen* **wir uns treffen?** (Shall we (would we like to) meet?) Here are the forms of **wollen** which you need to know:

ich	will	wir	wollen
du	willst	Sie/sie	wollen
er/sie/es/man	will		

Land und Leute

If you are arranging to do something outside, you need to know what the weather will be like. Look out or listen out for **der Wetterbericht** or **die Wettervorhersage** or **die Wetterkarte** on TV, the radio or in newspapers (**die Zeitung**); these will give you all the information you need!

U N I T 45 Towns and villages
Sightseeing

Vokabular

wann ist der Dom geöffnet?	when is the cathedral open?
kann man den Dom besichtigen?	can one visit the cathedral?
was gibt es dort zu sehen?	what's there to see?
die Altstadt	the old town
eine Schiffsfahrt	a boat trip
auf dem Rhein	on the Rhine
Köln	Cologne
montags bis freitags	Mondays until Fridays
geschlossen	closed
zwei Stunden	two hours

Dialog

tourist	Guten Tag. Ich bin für das Wochenende in Köln. Ich möchte die Stadt besichtigen – ich möchte viel sehen!
assistant	Also, Sie gehen am besten in die Altstadt.
tourist	In die Altstadt – was gibt es dort zu sehen?
assistant	Dort ist der Kölner Dom – er ist sehr berühmt.
tourist	Kann man den Dom besichtigen?
assistant	Ja, Sie können den Dom besichtigen.
tourist	Wann ist er geöffnet?
assistant	Er ist von montags bis freitags von 10 bis 18 Uhr geöffnet.
tourist	Und am Wochenende?
assistant	Am Wochenende ist der Dom geschlossen.
tourist	Was können Sie noch empfehlen? Eine Stadtrundfahrt?
assistant	Ja. Und Sie können eine Schiffsfahrt auf dem Rhein machen.
tourist	Eine Schiffsfahrt? Das ist interessant! Wie lange dauert die Fahrt?
assistant	Die Fahrt dauert zwei Stunden.
tourist	Vielen Dank!

Übungen

1 Tick the correct ending for each sentence.
(*Answers on page 130.*)

1. Am Wochenende ist der Dom
   a) besichtigen ☐
   b) geschlossen ☐

2. Eine Stadtrundfahrt ist sehr
   a) interessant ☐
   b) geöffnet ☐

3. Die Stadtrundfahrt
   a) ist von zehn bis 18 Uhr geöffnet ☐
   b) dauert eine Stunde ☐

4. Sie können eine Schiffsfahrt
   a) in die Altstadt machen ☐
   b) auf dem Rhein machen ☐

2 Look at the adverts below. Are the statements true or false? (*Answers on page 130.*)

> ## Der Dom in Münster
>
> | Montags bis freitags: | von elf bis halb acht geöffnet |
> |---|---|
> | Am Wochenende: | am Samstag von 10 Uhr bis 16 Uhr geöffnet |
> | | am Sonntag geschlossen |

> ## Stadtrundfahrt: Münster-Altstadt
>
> Samstags: 12 Uhr, 14.30 Uhr, 17 Uhr (zwei Stunden 30 Minuten)
> Sonntags: 13 Uhr, 16 Uhr (drei Stunden)

	true	false
1. The cathedral is only open Saturdays and during the week.	☐	☐
2. It's open from 11 until 8.30 during the week.	☐	☐
3. On Saturday it's open from 10 until 4.	☐	☐
4. The sightseeing tour goes through the new part of Münster.	☐	☐
5. The tour on Sunday is longer than the one on Saturday.	☐	☐
6. The last tour on Sunday starts at six o'clock.	☐	☐

3 Now you are in the tourist office. Practise saying the questions below in German. (*Answers on the recording and on page 130.*)

1. What is there to see?
2. What else can you recommend?
3. Can one visit the cathedral?
4. When is the cathedral open?
5. And when is it closed?

Tip

Here are all the forms of the modal verb **können** *(can)*:

ich	*kann*	wir	*können*
du	*kannst*	Sie/sie	*können*
er/sie/es/man	*kann*		

Land und Leute

The largest river in Germany and in Switzerland is **der Rhein** (the Rhine), and the largest river in Austria is **die Donau** (the Danube).

Weather

More about the weather

Vokabular

haben Sie jedes Jahr Schnee?	do you have snow every year?
das ist normal	that's normal
sechs Monate Schnee im Jahr	six months of snow each year
minus 30 oder 40 Grad	minus 30 or 40 degrees
meine Schwester	my sister
bei Ihnen	at yours
bei uns	at ours
nass	wet
auf Helgoland	on Helgoland
eine Insel	an island
in der Nordsee	in the North Sea
sicher	surely
immer	always
natürlich	certainly
manchmal	sometimes
meistens	most of the time

 ### Dialog

Herr Kunz	Darf ich vorstellen, Herr Braun: Frau Miller aus Kanada.
Herr Braun	Guten Abend, Frau Miller!
Frau Miller	Guten Abend, Herr Braun.
Herr Braun	Kanada – wie interessant! Meine Schwester wohnt auch in Kanada!
Frau Miller	Ja? Wo wohnt Ihre Schwester denn?
Herr Braun	Sie wohnt in Toronto. Und Sie, Frau Miller – wo wohnen Sie?
Frau Miller	Ich komme aus Calgary. Das ist im Norden.
Herr Kunz	In Kanada ist es sicher sehr kalt, nicht wahr?
Frau Miller	Ja, bei uns ist es im Winter immer sehr kalt – zu kalt!
Herr Kunz	Haben Sie jedes Jahr Schnee?
Frau Miller	Ja, natürlich – wir haben Schnee von November bis April.
Herr Kunz	Was? Sie haben sechs Monate Schnee im Jahr?
Frau Miller	Oh ja, das ist normal. Im Winter sind dort immer minus 30 oder 40 Grad. Und Sie, Herr Braun? Wie ist das Wetter bei Ihnen im Winter?
Herr Braun	Also, bei uns ist es nass – und windig.
Frau Miller	Wo wohnen Sie denn?
Herr Braun	Ich wohne auf Helgoland. Das ist eine kleine Insel in der Nordsee.
Frau Miller	Und wie ist das Wetter im Sommer?
Herr Braun	Im Sommer ist es manchmal sehr schön – aber meistens regnet es!

Übungen

1 Fill in the questionnaire for where you live.

		immer	manchmal	meistens
1.	Bei uns ist es im Winter zu kalt!			
2.	Im Winter haben wir Schnee.			
3.	Im Sommer ist es heiß, und es gibt Gewitter.			
4.	Im Herbst ist es neblig und nass.			

2 Listen to the dialogue and fill in the grid. (*Answers on page 130.*)

comes from	weather in summer		weather in winter	
	☐ hot	☐ rain	☐ too cold	☐ wet
	☐ too hot	☐ windy	☐ snow	☐ thunderstorms
	☐ sun	☐ wet	☐ windy	☐ rain

3 Now it's your turn to talk about the weather. Answer the questions using the information below. (*Answers on the recording and on page 130.*)

1. good evening – no, you're from England
2. so where does your daughter live?
3. you live in Newcastle – that's in the North
4. yes – where you are it's always very cold in the winter

Tip

Do you remember the various forms of the verb **haben**? Try filling in the gaps and check back with Unit 11 to see if you are right.

ich h _____ **du h** _____ **er/sie/es** _____ **wir** _____ **Sie/sie** _____

Land und Leute

Helgoland is just one the German islands off Northern Germany's coastline. Another popular – and very fashionable – **Insel** in the **Nordsee** is **Sylt**, which attracts the richest and most fashionable 'in-crowd' every summer.

Problems

Broken down

Vokabular

ich habe eine Panne	I've broken down
was ist los?	what's the problem?
ich habe eine Reifenpanne	I've got a puncture
die Scheinwerfer sind kaputt	the headlights don't work
der Motor ist kaputt	the engine doesn't work
bleiben Sie beim Auto	wait near the car
wir kommen sofort	we'll be there soon
kein Benzin	no petrol
die Autobahnabfahrt	the motorway exit
genau	exactly

Dialoge

mechanic	Guten Tag. Ja bitte?
customer 1	Ich habe eine Panne!
mechanic	Wo sind Sie?
customer 1	Auf der Landstraße 30 in Richtung Hamburg.
mechanic	Was ist los?
customer 1	Ich habe eine Reifenpanne. Und die Scheinwerfer sind kaputt.
mechanic	Bleiben Sie beim Auto. Wir kommen sofort.
mechanic	Ja? Kann ich helfen?
customer 2	Ja. Ich habe eine Panne. Die Scheinwerfer sind kaputt, und der Motor ist kaputt.
mechanic	Wo sind Sie genau?
customer 2	Ich bin auf der Autobahn 3 nicht weit von Lübeck.
mechanic	In der Nähe der Autobahnabfahrt Lübeck?
customer 2	Ja. Können Sie helfen?
mechanic	Ja. Bleiben Sie beim Auto!
customer 3	Guten Tag, ich bin auf der Bundestraße 12. Ich habe kein Benzin!
mechanic	Wo sind Sie?
customer 3	Nicht weit von Pinneberg in Richtung Hamburg.
mechanic	Ist gut. Bleiben Sie beim Auto!

Übungen

1 Match the phrases with the right illustrations. (*Answers on page 130.*)

1. Der Motor ist kaputt! a)   b)

2. Ich habe kein Benzin! a)   b)

3. Ich habe eine Reifenpanne! a)   b)

4. Die Scheinwerfer sind kaputt! a)   b)

2 Now it's your turn to speak. Say the phrases in German out loud. (*Answers on page 130.*)

1. I've broken down.
2. The engine doesn't work.
3. I've got a puncture.
4. The headlights don't work.
5. I've run out of petrol.

3 You've broken down on the road. Listen to the car mechanic's questions and answer in the pauses on the recording. (*Answers on page 130.*)

1. you've broken down
2. no, engine is not broken – no petrol
3. yes – and headlights don't work either
4. not far from Pinneberg – towards Hamburg
5. no – on motorway 1
6. near the exit
7. yes – can you help?

Tip

Here's a reminder of some modal verbs:

ich *muss*	er/sie/es *muss*	wir/Sie/sie *müssen*	kommen
ich *kann*	er/sie/es *kann*	wir/Sie/sie *können*	kommen
ich *soll*	er/sie/es *soll*	wir/Sie/sie *sollen*	kommen
ich *will*	er/sie/es *will*	wir/Sie/sie *wollen*	kommen

Land und Leute

When travelling by car in Germany, make sure your car insurance is up to date and that you have breakdown cover, too. In the case of an accident or emergency, the **ADAC** (the German equivalent of the AA/RAC) should be able to help you.

The present, the future and the past

Plans for tomorrow

Dialog

Frau Sommer Was machen Sie morgen, Herr Smith?

Herr Smith Morgen früh gehe ich in die Stadt. Ich will Andenken für meine Familie kaufen.

Frau Sommer Und am Nachmittag?

Herr Smith Am Nachmittag gehe ich ins Museum. Dort gibt es eine interessante Austellung.

Frau Sommer Und was machen Sie morgen abend?

Herr Smith Morgen abend gehe ich mit meiner Frau aus – wir wollen essen gehen.

Herr Klein Und Sie, Frau Sommer? Was machen Sie morgen?

Frau Sommer Morgen machen wir eine Wanderung in die Berge. Und am Abend treffen wir Freunde. Wir gehen in die Oper.

Herr Smith Und Sie, Herr Klein? Was machen Sie morgen?

Herr Klein Morgen früh ruhe ich mich aus!

Frau Sommer Und was machen Sie am Nachmittag?

Herr Klein Am Nachmittag mache ich einen Ausflug an den See.

Frau Sommer Machen Sie dort eine Schiffsfahrt?

Herr Klein Nein, ich mache einen Spaziergang.

Frau Sommer Und am Abend? Was machen Sie morgen abend?

Herr Klein Morgen abend gehe ich ins Kino.

Übungen

1 Make phrases with the words below. (*Answers on page 130.*)

1. meiner aus ich morgen Frau gehe mit abend .

2. in die morgen ich früh Stadt fahre .

3. nachmittag einen ich morgen mache Ausflug .

2 Read what Frau Müller and Herr Bayer have planned for tomorrow. Reorder the phrases to make their agenda for the next day. (*Answers on page 130.*)

1. Frau Müller
   a) Am Nachmittag gehe ich mit meinem Mann in die Stadt.
   b) Morgen abend gehe ich mit meiner Familie ins Theater.
   c) Morgen früh ruhe ich mich in meinem Hotelzimmer aus.

2. Herr Bayer
   a) Am Abend gehe ich mit meiner Frau aus.
   b) Morgen früh fahre ich mit dem Bus in die Stadt.
   c) Morgen nachmittag mache ich einen Ausflug.

3 You are talking about your plans for tomorrow. Listen to the questions and answer in the pauses on the recording according to the notes below. (*Answers on pages 130–1.*)

morning: excursion (walk to the lake)
afternoon: into town: museum + and you want to buy souvenirs!
evening: going out with wife – you want to go for a meal

Tip

Here is a list of words for the time of day:

heute	today	**morgen**	tomorrow
heute morgen	this morning	**morgen früh**	tomorrow morning
heute nachmittag	this afternoon	**morgen nachmittag**	tomorrow afternoon
heute abend	this evening	**morgen abend**	tomorrow evening
heute nacht	tonight	**morgen nacht**	tomorrow night

Land und Leute

When buying gifts and duty-free goods in Germany, make sure you know the customs and VAT regulations for your home country beforehand!

Self and others

Family

ein Foto von Ihrer Familie	a photo of your family
sympathisch	nice/kind
meine Eltern	my parents
noch andere Geschwister	other brothers and sisters
mein Bruder	my brother
Schwestern	sisters
verheiratet	married
geschieden	divorced
ledig	single
einen Hund	a dog
eine Katze	a cat

Dialog

Frau Klar	Haben Sie auch ein Foto von Ihrer Familie, Herr Sauer?
Herr Sauer	Ja, hier ... rechts – das ist meine Frau, Karin.
Herr Mohr	Ihre Frau sieht sehr sympathisch aus!
Herr Sauer	Und links – das ist meine Tochter Anna.
Herr Mohr	Wie alt ist Ihre Tochter?
Herr Sauer	Sie ist acht Jahre alt. Und neben meiner Tochter – das sind meine Eltern. Ja, mein Vater ist Schweizer, und meine Mutter kommt aus Österreich.
Frau Klar	Und wer ist der Mann dort links?
Herr Sauer	Das ist mein Bruder Ulrich. Er wohnt in München.
Frau Klar	Haben Sie noch andere Geschwister?
Herr Sauer	Ja, ich habe noch einen Bruder und zwei Schwestern. Sagen Sie, sind Sie verheiratet, Frau Klar?
Frau Klar	Nein, ich bin geschieden. Und Sie, Herr Mohr? Haben Sie Familie?
Herr Mohr	Nein, ich bin ledig – aber ich habe einen Hund und eine Katze. Das ist meine Familie!

Übungen

1   Read the questions and find the correct answers. (*Answers on page 131.*)

1. Haben Sie Familie?
2. Haben Sie einen Hund?
3. Sind Sie verheiratet?
4. Wo wohnen Ihre Eltern?

a) Nein, ich habe eine Katze.
b) Sie wohnen in Bonn.
c) Ja, ich habe zwei Söhne.
d) Nein, ich bin ledig.

2 A reporter has interviewed the famous German pop star Ricky Donner. Listen to the interview. Then fill in the gaps below. (*Answers on page 131.*)

Hallo, mein _____ ist Ricky Donner. Ich bin 29 Jahre _____, und ich wohne in München. Ich habe drei _____ und eine _____. Meine _____ wohnen in der Schweiz. Ich bin nicht _____, ich bin _____. Kinder? Nein, ich habe _____ Kinder – aber ich habe einen _____ und eine _____.

3 Now it's your turn to talk about your family. Listen to the questions on the recording and answer in the pauses with the information below. (*Answers on the recording and on page 131.*)

1. no, you're married – are you married?
2. yes, you have a son – 6 years old
3. yes, your daughter is 13 years old
4. yes, a brother; he lives in Berlin
5. your parents live in Hamburg

Tip

Here are singular and the plural words for 'brother/s' and 'sisters':

singular		plural
der Bruder	→	**die Brüder**
die Schwester	→	**die Schwestern**

Note that the word **Geschwister** (brothers and sisters) is always plural and never has an article.

Land und Leute

Germany is a nation of pet lovers, with the most popular animal being pet fish (80 milllion)! In second place are birds (8,8 million), in third place are cats (4,7 million) and in fourth place are dogs (4,5 million).

 **Food and drink**

Breakfast

Vokabular

zum Frühstück	for breakfast
Speck oder Schinken	bacon or ham
Eier	eggs
ein Spiegelei	a fried egg
ein gekochtes Ei	a boiled egg
(der) Toast	toast
(das) Brötchen	bread roll
(die) Marmelade	jam
(der) Honig	honey
(das) Müsli	muesli
eine Tasse Kakao	a cup of chocolate

 ### Dialog

waiter	Was möchten Sie zum Frühstück essen?
guest	Ja, also … haben Sie Speck oder Schinken?
waiter	Ja, wir haben Speck. Möchten Sie auch Eier?
guest	Ja, gern, ich möchte ein Spiegelei – und Toast, bitte.
waiter	Toast mit Honig und Marmelade?
guest	Ja, bitte. Und eine Tasse Kaffee.
waiter	Und was möchten Sie zum Frühstück essen?
guest 2	Toast mag ich nicht – Brötchen, bitte.
waiter	Brötchen mit Marmelade oder Honig?
guest 2	Nein, Brötchen und Aufschnitt und Käse, bitte.
waiter	Brötchen mit Aufschnitt und Käse. Und für Ihre Tochter?
guest 2	Haben Sie Müsli?
waiter	Ja, wir haben Müsli.
guest 2	Meine Tochter möchte Müsli mit Milch, ein gekochtes Ei – und eine Tasse Kakao.
waiter	Ihr Frühstück kommt sofort!

Übungen

Match the speech bubbles on the left with the menus on the right. (*Answers on page 131.*)

a) Frühstück 1
Müsli mit Milch
ein Brötchen mit Marmelade
Kaffee oder Tee

1. I don't want anything sweet for breakfast – I'd like a roll with ham and a fried egg with bacon.

b) Großes Frühstück 3
Müsli mit Milch
zwei Brötchen mit Käse und Honig
ein gekochtes Ei
Tee, Kaffee oder Kakao

2. I'd like some cereal and some rolls. I don't like eggs, though.

3 I'm very hungry – muesli, rolls with cheese and honey, an egg and a hot chocolate, please!

c)
Frühstück 2
ein Brötchen mit Käse/Schinken
ein Spiegelei mit Speck
Tee oder Kaffee

2 Listen to the dialogue and, in English, write down all the items of food being offered to the customer. (*Answers on page 131.*)

3 You are ordering your breakfast for tomorrow. Fill in the form in German using the information below. (*Answers on page 131.*)

1. a boiled egg
2. toast with honey
3. muesli with milk
4. two rolls with cold meats
5. a cup of coffee

Hotel Union – Frühstück
1.
2.
3.
4.
5.

Tip

You learned another new preposition in this unit, **für: für Ihre Tochter** (for your daughter). Do you remember that there are two different rules for prepositions (see Unit 40)? The same rules apply when prepositions are used with the German for 'my', 'your' (**mein(e), Ihr(e)**):

der Mann → für *den* Mann
die Tochter → für die Tochter
das Frühstück → für das Frühstück

Ihr Mann → für *Ihren* Mann
Ihre Tochter → für Ihre Tochter
Ihr Frühstück → für Ihr Frühstück

Land und Leute

Here are some other items of food you might find on a German breakfast menu:

das Rührei	scrambled egg
die Cornflakes	cornflakes
die Butter/Margarine	butter/margarine
das Vollkornbrot	wholegrain bread
das Schwarzbrot	rye bread
der Kräuter-/Früchtetee	herbal/fruit tea
der Apfelsaft	apple juice

Shopping

More clothes

Vokabular

kann ich … anprobieren?	can I try … on?
ist jetzt sehr modern	is very fashionable now
einen Rock	a skirt
einen Mantel	a coat
im Sonderangebot	in the sales/reduced
zu bunt	too colourful
in Lila	in purple
eine Nummer größer	a size larger
in Grau	in grey
die Farbe	the colour
zu kurz	too short
länger	longer

Dialog

customer Guten Tag, ich suche einen Rock – und einen Mantel für meinen Mann.

assistant Gern – welche Größe?

customer Größe 42 für mich – und Größe 46 für meinen Mann.

assistant Hier – dieser Rock ist Größe 42 – und er ist im Sonderangebot.

customer Nein, der Rock ist zu bunt – haben Sie den Rock auch in Lila?

assistant Ja, hier – bitte.

customer Der Rock gefällt mir. Kann ich den Rock anprobieren?

assistant Ja, natürlich – dort links. … Passt der Rock?

customer Nein, er ist zu klein. Haben Sie den Rock eine Nummer größer?

assistant Hier, bitte.

customer Ja, den Rock nehme ich. Und wo finde ich Mäntel?

assistant Dort drüben. Dieser Mantel in Grau ist sehr schön! Grau ist jetzt sehr modern.

customer Nein, die Farbe gefällt mir nicht. Haben Sie den Mantel auch in Braun?

assistant Hier, bitte.

customer Nein, dieser Mantel ist zu kurz. Aber dieser hier ist länger! Ja, diesen Mantel nehme ich auch – wo ist die Kasse, bitte?

assistant Die Kasse ist dort drüben.

Übungen

1 Read the dialogue and reorder it. (*Answers on page 131.*)

1. Welche Größe?
2. Hier, dieser Rock ist im Sonderangebot.
3. Ja, dort rechts.
4. Größe 42.
5. Guten Tag, ich suche einen Rock.
6. Kann ich ihn anprobieren?

2   Read the dialogue below. Then decide whether the statements below are true or false. (*Answers on page 131.*)

Cross reference with units: 3 15 27 39

Man   *Assistant*

Guten Tag, ich suche eine Jeans.   Gern – welche Größe?

Größe 44.   Größe 44 – hier, diese Jeans ist im Sonderangebot.

Nein, die Farbe gefällt mir nicht. Haben Sie die Jeans auch in Schwarz?   Ja.

Haben Sie die Jeans eine Nummer größer?   Gefällt Ihnen die Jeans?

Nein. Diese Jeans passt – aber sie ist zu bunt.

	true	false
1. The man is looking for a pair of jeans in size 44.	☐	☐
2. The first pair is in the sale.	☐	☐
3. He doesn't like the fit of the first pair of trousers.	☐	☐
4. The second pair is too large.	☐	☐
5. The last pair is too colourful.	☐	☐

3   Listen to the shop assistant and the prompts in English. Respond in the pauses on the recording. (*Answers on the recording and on page 131.*)

1. say you're looking for a coat
2. size 40, please
3. you don't like the colour
4. no, it's too colourful – do you have this coat in black?
5. no, it's too small – do you have this coat in a larger size?
6. no, this coat is too short

Tip

Note the forms:

Es gefällt mir/Ihnen/dir.   I like it (it pleases me)/you like it.
Sie gefallen mir/Ihnen/dir.   I like them (they please me)/you like them.
(**Ihnen** = polite, **dir** = informal)

Land und Leute

Every shop and department store in Germany offers goods in the sales twice a year: look out for **der Sommerschlussverkauf/SSV** (the summer sales) and der **Winterschlussverkauf/WSV** (the winter sales) while you're in Germany!

UNIT 52 Directions

'How do I get to ...?'

Vokabular

ich bin fremd hier	I don't live here
zur Jugendherberge	to the youth hostel
zu Fuß	on foot
den Berg hoch	up the hill
bis zum Schloss	as far as the palace/castle
durch den Wald	through the forest
das Freibad	the open-air swimming pool
die Querstraße	the crossroads
die Drogerie	the chemist's
wieder	again

Dialog

tourist	Entschuldigen Sie! Ich bin fremd hier – wie komme ich am besten zur Jugendherberge?
passer-by	Zur Jugendherberge – sind Sie zu Fuß?
tourist	Ja, ich bin zu Fuß. Ist es weit?
passer-by	Nein, zu Fuß ungefähr zehn Minuten. Also: Sie gehen hier rechts den Berg hoch – bis zum Schloss.
tourist	Rechts den Berg hoch – bis zum Schloss.
passer-by	Ja. Beim Schloss gehen Sie links – durch den Wald. Hinter dem Wald ist das Freibad.
tourist	Das Freibad – ja. Und dann?
passer-by	Dann gehen Sie rechts am Parkplatz vorbei – bis zur nächsten Querstraße.
tourist	Ich gehe rechts bis zur nächsten Querstraße ...
passer-by	Sie gehen dann wieder rechts und über die Brücke. Die Jugendherberge ist gleich neben der Brücke.
tourist	Neben der Brücke – vielen Dank. Ach ja, und ich suche eine Drogerie. Wo finde ich die nächste Drogerie?
passer-by	Also, Sie gehen geradeaus bis zur Post. An der Post gehen Sie links – bis zum Marktplatz. Dort ist die nächste Drogerie.

Übungen

1 Read the phrases below and fill in the missing words with the help of the illustrations. (*Answers on page 131.*)

1. Sie gehen durch den _____ .

2. Sind Sie zu ____ ?

3. Dann gehen Sie bis zum _____ .

4. Wie komme ich am besten zur _____ ?

5. Das _____ ist neben dem Parkplatz.

6. Wo finde ich die nächste _____ ?

Cross reference with units: 4 16 28 40

2 Listen to the dialogue. Are the statements below true or false? (*Answers on page 131.*)

	true	false
1. The tourist is asking for the way to the youth hostel.	☐	☐
2. She has to go over the bridge to the chemist's.	☐	☐
3. Then left to the next crossroads.	☐	☐
4. Then she has to go past the forest.	☐	☐
5. After that, she has to go up the hill and turn right at the castle.	☐	☐
6. The youth hostel is right behind the swimming pool.	☐	☐

3 Now you have to ask for directions. Using the English prompts below, ask the relevant questions. (*Answers on page 131.*)

1. excuse me – I don't live here
2. what's the best way to the youth hostel?
3. I'm on foot – is it far?
4. where is the swimming-pool?
5. and where is the castle?
6. where is the nearest pharmacy?

Tip

Note that the word order in German for directions like 'right again' is different:

Then you go *right again*.	→	**Sie gehen dann *wieder rechts*.**
1 2		2 1

Land und Leute

If you are planning a hiking holiday in Germany, **Jugendherbergen** (youth hostels) offer very cheap and comfortable accommodation, quite often to be found in old buildings like stable houses or castles and set in picturesque surroundings.

Numbers

Telephone numbers

Vokabular

Firma Bergmann!	(Company) Bergmann!
am Apparat	speaking
Sander hier	Sander speaking
ich möchte gern ... sprechen	I'd like to speak to ...
... ist im Moment nicht da	... is not here at the moment
... ist in einer Besprechung	... is in a meeting
soll ... Sie zurückrufen?	should ... call you back?
könnte ich bitte ... sprechen?	could I speak to ... ?
ich verbinde Sie	I'll put you through
zwo	two (used on the telephone for clarity)
Ihre Faxnummer	your fax number

Dialoge

Herr Greve	Guten Morgen, Firma Bergmann, Greve am Apparat.
Frau Sander	Guten Morgen, Sander hier. Ich möchte gerne Herrn Rau sprechen.
Herr Greve	Es tut mir leid, Herr Rau ist im Moment nicht da. Er ist in einer Besprechung.
Frau Sander	Wann ist er wieder im Büro?
Herr Greve	Das weiß ich leider nicht. Soll er Sie zurückrufen?
Frau Sander	Ja, bitte. Meine Telefonnummer ist Köln 0221 – 60 25 84.
Herr Greve	0221 – 60 25 84. Vielen Dank, Frau Sander. Auf Wiederhören!
Frau Sander	Auf Wiederhören!
Herr Greve	Guten Morgen, Firma Bergmann, Greve!
Herr Klar	Guten Morgen, mein Name ist Klar. Könnte ich bitte Frau Dallmeyer sprechen?
Herr Greve	Einen Moment – ich verbinde Sie.
Herr Klar	Danke. Ach – ich habe noch eine Frage: Wie ist Ihre Faxnummer, bitte?
Herr Greve	Unsere Faxnummer ist Dortmund 0231 – 33 64 869.
Herr Klar	0231 – 33 64 869. Vielen Dank!

Übungen

1 Match the phrases on the left with those on the right.
(*Answers on page 131.*)

1. Soll sie Sie zurückrufen?
2. Ich möchte gern Frau Kaiser sprechen.
3. Guten Morgen, Sauer am Apparat!
4. Wann ist sie wieder im Büro?
5. Könnte ich bitte Herrn Uhle sprechen?

a) Einen Moment – ich verbinde Sie.
b) Guten Morgen – Ahlers hier.
c) Ja, bitte. Meine Telefonnummer ist 76 54 67.
d) Es tut mir leid – sie ist im Moment nicht da.
e) Das weiß ich leider nicht.

2 Read the transcript of a message on Frau Baumann's answerphone. Fill in the gaps with the words below. (*Answers on page 131.*)

Guten Tag, mein _____ ist Johann Müller. Es ist _____ vor elf, und ich_____ gern Frau Karla Baumann _____ . Meine _____ ist Hamburg 040 90 56 78. _____ Faxnummer ist 040 90 57 94. Auf _____

| möchte | Wiederhören | Viertel | Telefonnummer | Name | sprechen | Meine |

3 Now it's your turn to give and ask for phone and fax numbers. Listen to the receptionist and respond in the pauses using the notes below. (*Answers on the recording and on page 131.*)

1. yes, please; my phone number is 0360 67 03 24
2. my fax number is 0360 44 77 58
3. I've got another question: what's your fax number, please?
4. 0531 69 82 74; thanks – good bye

Tip

You learned a new verb form in this unit: **könnte** (could) – **könnte ich bitte Frau Dallmeyer sprechen? Könnte** is the polite form of the modal verb **können (ich kann).** As for all modal verbs, the second verb goes at the end of the sentence. Here are the other forms of **könnte**:

ich	könn*te*	wir	könn*ten*
du	könn*test*	Sie/sie	könn*ten*
er/sie/es	könn*te*		

Land und Leute

If you ring a person or a company in Germany, you might get the answerphone – **der Anrufbeantworter**. Don't be afraid – simply leave your message (**die Nachricht**) after the beep (**nach dem Ton**)! More and more Germans now carry mobile phones, too; these have an English name – **das Handy!**

Public transport

Buying a railway ticket

Vokabular

Raucher	smoking
Nichtraucher	non-smoking
einen Fensterplatz	a window seat
direkt	straight through
von welchem Gleis?	from which platform?

Dialog

tourist Was kostet eine Fahrkarte nach München, bitte?
clerk Erster Klasse?
tourist Ja, erster Klasse.
clerk Einfach kostet 253 Mark, und hin und zurück kostet 295 Mark.
tourist Das ist aber teuer! Und was kostet eine Fahrkarte zweiter Klasse?
clerk Zweiter Klasse kostet einfach 199 Mark, und hin und zurück kostet 261 Mark.
tourist Dann möchte ich eine Fahrkarte zweiter Klasse – hin und zurück, bitte.
clerk Gern. Raucher oder Nichtraucher?
tourist Nichtraucher, bitte.
clerk Und möchten Sie einen Fensterplatz?
tourist Ja, bitte. Hier – 500 Mark.
clerk Danke. So – 261 Mark – Sie bekommen 239 Mark zurück.
tourist Danke. Muss ich umsteigen?
clerk Nein, der Zug fährt direkt.
tourist Und wann fährt der nächste Zug?
clerk Der nächste Zug fährt um 18 Uhr 55.
tourist Und von welchem Gleis?
clerk Von Gleis 16.
tourist Vielen Dank!

Übungen

1 Put the dialogue at the ticket office in the right order.
(*Answers on page 131.*)

1. Und von welchem Gleis?
2. Nichtraucher.
3. Einfach oder hin und zurück?
4. Ja, bitte. Muss ich umsteigen?
5. Hin und zurück, bitte – zweiter Klasse.
6. Gleis 3.
7. 255 Mark. Raucher oder Nichtraucher?
8. Und möchten Sie eine Fensterplatz?
9. Nein, der Zug fährt direkt.
10. Was kostet eine Fahrkarte nach Berlin?

2 Listen to the dialogue and fill in the details. (*Answers on page 131.*)

ticket to: _____ ☐ first class   ☐ single
                           ☐ second class ☐ return
price (single)_____ ☐ smoking   ☐ window seat
price (return)_____ ☐ non-smoking ☐ no window seat

3 Look at the illustrations and match them with the right phrases. (*Answers on page 131.*)

1.   2

3.    4.

5.    6.

a) Zweiter Klasse, bitte.
b). Wann fährt der nächste Zug?
c) Nichtraucher, bitte.
d) Hin und zurück.
e) Von welchem Gleis?
f) Was kostet eine Fahrkarte nach Berlin, bitte?

Tip

von is another preposition. Note how it is used:

das Gleis → **welches Gleis?** → *von welchem Gleis?*

Land und Leute

As environmentally-aware countries, Germany and Switzerland are eager for their citizens to leave their cars at home and use public transport instead. The local public transport systems are heavily subsidised and offer attractive incentives for travellers who decide to switch from using their cars to taking buses, trams or underground trains.

 **Accommodation**

At the camp site

Vokabular

gibt es einen Campingplatz?	is there a camp site?
gibt es einen Spielraum?	is there a games room?
haben Sie Platz?	do you have space?
die Anmeldung	the reception
für ein Zelt	for a tent
für einen Wohnwagen	for a caravan
eine Waschmaschine	a washing maschine
neben dem Waschraum	next to the washroom
hier in der Nähe	in the vicinity
kein Problem	no problem

 ### Dialog

tourist	Entschuldigung, gibt es einen Campingplatz hier in der Nähe?
passer-by	Ja, nehmen Sie die erste Straße rechts. Dort ist der Campingplatz.
tourist	... Wo ist denn die Anmeldung? Ah, dort drüben.
assistant	Ja bitte – kann ich Ihnen helfen?
tourist	Ja. Haben Sie Platz für fünf Nächte?
assistant	Für ein Zelt?
tourist	Nein, für einen Wohnwagen.
assistant	Und für wie viele Personen?
tourist	Für vier Personen – mein Mann, meine zwei Kinder und ich.
assistant	Ja, wir haben Platz für Sie – kein Problem.
tourist	Sagen Sie, gibt es auch einen Spielraum?
assistant	Ja, der Spielraum ist dort links.
tourist	Und eine Waschmaschine – gibt es eine Waschmaschine?
assistant	Ja, natürlich, die Waschmaschine ist neben dem Waschraum.
tourist	Vielen Dank!

Übungen

1 Match up a word from 1. to 6. with one from a) to f) to make a new word. There are several possibilities. (*Answers on page 131.*)

1. WASCH	a) PLATZ
2. WOHN	b) RAUM
3. SPIEL	c) MASCHINE
4. AN	d) WAGEN
5. CAMPING	e) RAUM
6. WASCH	f) MELDUNG

2 Read the sentences and choose the correct ending. (*Answers on page 131.*)

1. Haben Sie Platz
   a) für ein Zelt? ☐
   b) für eine Waschmaschine? ☐

2. Gibt es einen
   a) Wohnwagen? ☐
   b) Spielraum? ☐

3. Die Anmeldung ist neben dem
   a) Waschraum. ☐
   b) Campingplatz. ☐

4. Ich habe Platz für zwei
   a) Waschmaschinen. ☐
   b) Nächte. ☐

3 Listen to the recording and reply to the campsite receptionist using the information below. (*Answers on the recording and on page 131.*)

1.    2.   3.

4.   5.

Tip

Note the following plurals:

der Campingplatz	**die Campingplätze**
das Zelt	**die Zelte**
der Wohnwagen	**die Wohnwagen**
die Person	**die Personen**
die Waschmaschine	**die Waschmaschinen**
der Waschraum	**die Waschräume**

Land und Leute

Camping is very popular in Germany with a lot of families who have their own **Wohnwagen** or **ein Wohnmobil** (camper van). Popular camping areas are the coastal regions of **die Nordsee** (the North Sea) and **die Ostsee** (the Baltic Sea), and, in the South, **der Schwarzwald** (the Black Forest) and **der Bayrische Wald** (the Bavarian Forest).

Hobbies and pastimes

Going on an excursion

Vokabular

wo müssen wir warten?	where do we have to wait?
ich möchte ein Boot leihen	I'd like to hire a boat
die Karten	tickets
Kinderermäßigung	concession for children
ein Tretboot	a pedal boat
ein Ruderboot	a rowing boat
auf dem See	on the lake
wie oft?	how often?
jede Stunde	every hour
in der Schlange	in the queue
pro Stunde	per hour

Dialoge

customer	Guten Tag, wir möchten eine Schiffsfahrt auf dem See machen.
assistant	Gern – die Fahrt dauert zwei Stunden.
customer	Wie oft fährt das Schiff?
assistant	Jede Stunde – die nächste Fahrt ist um 15 Uhr 45. Möchten Sie Karten?
customer	Ja bitte. Was kostet eine Karte?
assistant	Acht Mark fünfzig.
customer	Gibt es auch Kinderermäßigung?
assistant	Ja, eine Kinderkarte kostet fünf Mark.
customer	Gut, zwei Karten für mich und meinen Mann – und eine Kinderkarte bitte.
assistant	22 Mark bitte.
customer	Hier, bitte. Wo müssen wir warten?
assistant	Dort drüben – in der Schlange.
customer 2	Entschuldigen Sie – ich möchte ein Boot leihen.
assistant	Möchten Sie ein Tretboot oder ein Ruderboot leihen?
customer 2	Ein Ruderboot, bitte. Was kostet eine Fahrt?
assistant	Sieben Mark pro Stunde. Möchten Sie ein Boot für zwei Personen?
customer 2	Ja, bitte. Hier sind sieben Mark.
assistant	Danke. Ihr Boot ist die Nummer sieben – es ist grün.

Übungen

1 Read the signs below. Are the statements true or false? (*Answers on page 131.*)

Schiffsfahrt auf dem See	
Jede Stunde: 10 Uhr 15 – 16 Uhr 15	
(Die Fahrt dauert 90 Minuten.)	
Karte:	9 Mark 50
Kinderermäßigung:	6 Mark

BOOTE – BOOTE – BOOTE	
Tretboot für eine Fahrt	1 – 2 Personen 8 Mark pro Stunde
Ruderboot eine Fahrt	für 1 – 4 Personen 11 Mark pro Stunde

	true	false
1. The boat trip takes 1 hour, and there is one every hour.	☐	☐
2. The boats depart from quarter to 11 to quarter to four.	☐	☐
3. A ticket costs 9 Marks.	☐	☐
4. A children's ticket is 6 Mark.	☐	☐
5. One can hire a pedal boat for one to four people.	☐	☐
6. A trip with a rowing boat is more expensive than one with a pedal boat.	☐	☐

2 Listen to the announcement and fill in the grid. (*Answers on page 131.*)

boat trips	
from	to
how long	how often
times	ticket
children	
boat hire – rowing boat	
how many people	price
boat hire – pedal boat	
how many people	price

3 Now it's your turn to pay for your tickets. Listen to the assistant telling you the prices (which are also shown below). Add them up and say the total out loud in the pause. (*Answers on the recording and on page 131.*)

1. DM 7 + DM 22   2. DM 8 + DM 12 + DM 5   3. DM 9 + DM 15 + DM 13

Tip

The German for 'how often?', **wie oft?**, follows the same rules as all other question words: just remember to put the question words at the beginning of the sentence followed by the verb:

Wie oft	*fährt*	*das* **Schiff?**	How often does the ship go?
question word	verb		

Land und Leute

The largest lake in Germany is **der Bodensee** (Lake Constance) in **Baden-Württemberg**. Switzerland's largest lake is der **Genfer See** (Lake Geneva), and the largest lake in Austria is **der Neusiedler See**.

Towns and villages

Staying with friends

Vokabular

Sie können bei uns übernachten	you can stay with us
wann kommen Sie in Berlin an?	when do you arrive in Berlin?
am ... müssen wir wieder zurück	we have to go back on ...
ich hole Sie ab	I'll pick you up
ich freue mich schon sehr auf Ihren Besuch	I'm very much looking forward to your visit
das ist sehr nett	that's very nice
mit dem Flugzeug	by plane
wirklich	really

Dialog

Herr Meier Meier!

Herr Smith Guten Tag, Herr Meier! Smith hier – Dave Smith.

Herr Meier Guten Tag, Herr Smith! Wie geht es Ihnen?

Herr Smith Danke, sehr gut. Wie ist das Wetter in Berlin?

Herr Meier Gut. Sind Sie zu Hause in Manchester, Herr Smith?

Herr Smith Ja. Aber meine Frau und ich – wir kommen im August nach Berlin. Können wir uns treffen?

Herr Meier Ja, natürlich, gern! Sie können auch gern bei uns übernachten!

Herr Smith Wirklich? Haben Sie Platz für uns?

Herr Meier Ja, kein Problem – wir haben ein großes Haus!

Herr Smith Danke, das ist sehr nett!

Herr Meier Sagen Sie, wann kommen Sie in Berlin an?

Herr Smith Also, wir kommen am 14. August an. Am 17. August müssen wir wieder zurück nach Manchester.

Herr Meier Kommen Sie mit dem Flugzeug?

Herr Smith Ja, wir kommen mit dem Flugzeug.

Herr Meier Kein Problem! Ich hole Sie dann vom Flughafen ab! Ich freue mich schon sehr auf Ihren Besuch!

Übungen

1 Make phrases with the words below. (*Answers on page 131.*)

1. in | Sie | wann | an | Berlin | kommen ?

2. mich | Besuch | ich | auf | freue | Ihren | sehr | schon .

3. bei | übernachten | Sie | uns | können .

4. mit | Sie | dem | Flugzeug | kommen ?

5. zurück | am | wir | müssen | 5. Mai | wieder .

2 Listen to the dialogue and answer the questions below. (*Answers on page 131.*)

1. Where do Herr Kaiser and his wife live?
2. In which month will Frau Meier and her husband be in their town?
3. What is Herr Kaiser offering?
4. What are their arrival and departure dates?
5. How are they getting there?
6. Where is Herr Kaiser picking them up from?

3 Complete the phrases in German using the information below. (*Answers on page 131.*)

1. Can we meet?
   Können wir _____ _____ ?
2. Have you got space for us?
   Haben Sie _____ _____ uns?
3. We are coming by train.
   Wir kommen _____ _____ _____
4. I'm looking forward to it!
   Ich _____ _____ schon _____ !

Tip

As in English, words like **wirklich** (really) are much used in spoken German – they add a natural, authentic feel to the language. You already know:

| **aber** | but | → | **Das ist *aber* teuer!** |
| **auch** | also | → | **Sie können *auch* bei uns übernachten!** |

There are other 'filler words' which don't add any new meaning, but which are also very important in spoken German. Here are some that you already know: **ach ja** (I see/of course), **ja, also …** (yes, so …).

Land und Leute

If you arrive by plane (**das Flugzeug**) in Germany, the easiest way is to take a taxi (**ein Taxi**) from the airport to your destination. German taxis are usually cream-coloured Mercedes with a yellow and black taxi sign on the roof. It is customary to give the driver a tip when you pay. And if you need a receipt for the journey, ask the driver for **eine Quittung, bitte!**

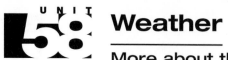

Weather

More about the weather

Vokabular

ich kenne das	I know that
Heuschnupfen	hayfever
starkes Asthma	severe asthma
allergisch gegen Pollen	allergic to (against) pollen
gegen Hunde und Katzen	to (against) dogs and cats
gegen Pferde	to (against) horses
wieso nicht?	why not?
über 29 Grad	more than 29 degrees
wie ärgerlich!	how annoying!
nämlich	you see
furchtbar	awful
schon	already
den ganzen Tag	all day

Dialog

Frau Rau	Hallo, Herr Schmidt, ich komme morgen um 16 Uhr in München an. Sagen Sie – wie ist das Wetter in München?
Herr Schmidt	Es ist sehr heiß – über 29 Grad, und es ist sehr windig.
Frau Rau	Oh nein, wie ärgerlich! Heiß und windig – das ist nicht gut für mich.
Herr Schmidt	Wieso nicht?
Frau Rau	Ich habe nämlich Heuschnupfen – ich bin allergisch gegen Pollen.
Herr Schmidt	Ja, das ist im Sommer ein Problem. Ich kenne das – im Sommer habe ich starkes Asthma.
Frau Rau	Sind Sie auch gegen Pollen allergisch?
Herr Schmidt	Nein, ich bin gegen Hunde und Katzen allergisch.
Frau Rau	Ja, mein Mann ist auch gegen Hunde allergisch – gegen Hunde und Pferde.
Herr Schmidt	Und wie ist das Wetter bei Ihnen in Hamburg, Frau Rau?
Frau Rau	Furchtbar! Es ist nass und kalt – es regnet schon den ganzen Tag!

Übungen

1 People are allergic to many different things. Complete the sentences with the most likely word. (*Answers on page 131.*)

Knoblauch   Aspirin   Milch   Hausstaub

1. Ist _____ im Salat? Ich bin allergisch gegen _____ .

2. Ich habe Kopfschmerzen, aber _____ kann ich nicht nehmen.

3. Kaffee mit _____? Ach nein, ich bin allergisch gegen _____ .

4. Ich lese nicht gern alte Bücher. Ich bin allergisch gegen _____ .

2 Listen to the dialogue at the doctor's surgery. Are the statements true or false? (*Answers on page 131.*)

	true	false
1. The patient has got a headache and his throat hurts.	☐	☐
2. He thinks he has got hayfever.	☐	☐
3. Hayfever is a problem in spring, according to the doctor.	☐	☐
4. The doctor has severe asthma at this time of the year.	☐	☐
5. She's allergic to pollen.	☐	☐
6. The patient has to take the tablets twice a day.	☐	☐

3 Now it's your turn. You are going to Hamburg tomorrow and want to know about the weather. Complete the conversation in German using the English prompts below. (*Answers on the recording and on pages 131–2.*)

1. awful! – it is wet and cold!
2. no, it's not windy; and how is the weather in Hamburg?
3. oh no – I've got hayfever, you see
4. yes, I'm allergic to pollen, and cats

Tip

Note that the preposition **gegen** (against) is always used with a plural noun and doesn't have an article when used in phrases like 'I am allergic to/against':

Ich bin allergisch *gegen* Pferde.   (das Pferd)

Land und Leute

Der Föhn is a strong warm wind which frequently blows through areas to the North and South of the Alps – especially in summer. People with asthma and allergies suffer from it especially.

UNIT 59 Problems

Accidents and emergencies

Vokabular

was ist passiert?	what happened?
wie geht es dem Radfahrer?	how is the cyclist?
sind Sie verletzt?	are you hurt?
mein linker Arm ist gebrochen	I've broken my left arm
bewegen Sie sich nicht!	don't move!
rufen Sie einen Krankenwagen!	call an ambulance!
ein Unfall	an accident
mein rechtes Bein	my right leg
mein Rücken	my back
sein Herz	his heart
der Schock	the shock
einen Herzanfall	a heart attack
schnell!	quickly!

Dialog

passer-by	Ein Unfall! Was ist passiert? Wie geht es dem Radfahrer? Sind Sie verletzt?
cyclist	Au – mein Bein – mein rechtes Bein tut weh! Und mein Arm – mein linker Arm ist gebrochen!
passer-by	Und Sie – Sind Sie verletzt? Wo tut es weh?
woman driver	Mein Kopf tut weh – und mein Rücken – Au!
passer-by	Bewegen Sie sich nicht! Schnell – einen Krankenwagen – rufen Sie einen Krankenwagen!
cyclist	Ja – und rufen Sie die Polizei!
passer-by	Und Ihr Mann – wie geht es Ihrem Mann? Ist er verletzt?
woman driver	Sein Herz – der Schock – oh nein, mein Mann hat einen Herzanfall!
passer-by	Der Krankenwagen kommt sofort!

Übungen

1 Match up the sentences. (*Answers on page 132.*)

1. Rufen Sie
2. Mein Arm
3. Mein Mann
4. Mein rechtes Bein

a) tut weh!
b) einen Krankenwagen!
c) ist gebrochen!
d) hat einen Herzanfall!

2 Listen to the three dialogues. Then fill in a police report for each accident. (*Answers on page 132.*)

Accident 1

What kind of injury/injuries? ....

Which emergency service was called out? ....

Accident 2

Who was injured? ....

What kind of injury/injuries? ....

Which emergency service was called out? ....

Accident 3

Who was injured? ....

What kind of injury/injuries? ....

Which emergency service was called out? ....

3 Now it's your turn. Say each of the phrases below in German. (*Answers on page 132.*)

1. are you hurt?
2. quickly – call an ambulance
3. don't move
4. my left arm hurts!
5. my right leg is broken
6. my back hurts

Tip

Remember to form commands or instructions in German by putting the verb at the beginning of the sentence:

Rufen **Sie einen Krankenwagen!** → **Sie** *rufen* **einen Krankenwagen.**
Bewegen **Sie sich nicht!** → **Sie** *bewegen* **sich nicht.**

Land und Leute

The German emergency numbers are 110 for the police and ambulance and 112 for the fire brigade (**die Feuerwehr**).

The present, the future and the past

Arranging a meal

Vokabular

ich möchte Sie zum Essen einladen	I'd like to invite you for a meal (and to pay!)
ich esse kein Fleisch	I don't eat meat
ein Steakhaus	a steak house
ein Vegetarier	a vegetarian
ein italienisches Restaurant	an Italian restaurant
chinesische Küche	Chinese cuisine
vegetarische Gerichte	vegetarian food
nicht so gerne	not that much
mein letzter Tag	my last day
warum?	why?

Dialog

Herr Dyer	Guten Tag, Frau Berger – Peter Dyer hier.
Frau Berger	Hallo, Herr Dyer! Wann fahren Sie nach Amerika zurück?
Herr Dyer	Morgen früh. Heute ist mein letzter Tag in Hamburg. Sagen Sie, haben Sie und Ihr Mann heute abend Zeit?
Frau Berger	Ja, warum?
Herr Dyer	Ich möchte Sie zum Essen einladen.
Frau Berger	Danke, Herr Dyer! Gerne!
Herr Dyer	Wo möchten Sie essen gehen?
Frau Berger	Wie wäre es mit italienisch? Am Marktplatz ist ein neues italienisches Restaurant.
Herr Dyer	Nein, italienisch esse ich nicht so gerne.
Frau Berger	Essen Sie gern Fleisch? Am Rathaus ist ein Steakhaus.
Herr Dyer	Nein, ich bin Vegetarier. Ich esse kein Fleisch.
Frau Berger	Wie wäre es mit chinesisch?
Herr Dyer	Nein, es tut mir leid – chinesische Küche mag ich nicht.
Frau Berger	Ich weiß – in der Innenstadt gibt es ein türkisches Restaurant.
Herr Dyer	Ja, dort gibt es auch vegetarische Gerichte!

Übungen

1 Read the statements and and look at the restaurant signs on the right. Find the right restaurant for each person. (*Answers on page 132.*)

1.
Frau Meier doesn't eat meat.

a)

Das Steakhaus am Markt

Heute:
Schnitzel mit Pommes
frites und Salat   15,50 DM

2.
Herr Klar loves Far Eastern cuisine.

b)

Cross reference with units:

> Jeden Mittwoch:
> *Italienische Küche*
> *Pizza, Spaghetti ...*

> Das Vegetariercafé
> • Salat •
> • Pizza mit Tomaten und Käse •
> • Müslikuchen •

3.
Fräulein Rau likes to eat traditional meat dishes.

c)

4.
Jan Sauer loves Mediterranean food.

d)

> NEU:
> *Das Chinesische Restaurant*
> *Jeden Tag 18–23 Uhr*

2 Read the phrases on the left and choose the correct endings on the right. (*Answers on page 132.*)

1. Ich möchte Sie gerne zum
2. Wie wäre es mit
3. Chinesische Küche
4. Ich esse kein
5. Vegetarische Gerichte

a) mag ich nicht.
b) esse ich nicht so gerne.
c) Essen einladen.
d) italienisch?
e) Fleisch.

3 Take part in a telephone conversation with Herr Berger using the information below. (*Answers on the recording and on page 132.*)

1. Good evening, Herr Berger – are you free this evening?
2. I'd like to invite you for a meal.
3. Where would you like to go for a meal?
4. No – I don't eat meat. I'm a vegetarian.
5. No – I'm sorry. I don't like Turkish cuisine.
6. No, I don't like eating Chinese (food) that much.
7. Yes – there are vegetarian dishes available too!

Tip

Note that when you say 'I am a vegetarian' in German, you do not use the article 'a': **Ich bin Vegetarier.** For the female noun, you simply add -**in** at the end: **Ich bin Vegetarierin.**

Land und Leute

If you are a vegetarian and don't eat fish, you would say **ich esse keinen Fisch**. And if you want to let people know that you are a diabetic, you can say **ich esse keinen Zucker** or **ich bin Diabetiker/in**. A lot of Germans are vegetarian these days, and almost all restaurants cater for this growing trend – so you should not have any problems in finding healthy vegetarian or simply meat-free dishes while sampling the German cuisine!

Herzlichen Glückwunsch! – many congratulations on finishing the course!

Answers

1 1 1. c); 2. d); 3. b); 4. a) **2** 1. Ich bin Herr Peters. 2. Wie heißen Sie? 3. Auf Wiedersehen! 4. Ich heiße Frau Meier. 5. Guten Tag! 6. Ich heiße Herr Sauer. 7. Wie geht es Ihnen? **3** 1. Guten Tag. 2. Ich heiße Herr/Frau ... 3. Danke, gut. 4. Auf Wiedersehen.

2 1 1. b); 2. c); 3. a) **2** small beer; white wine – small; to eat: yes **3** 1. Ein Glas Wein, bitte. 2. Rot, bitte. 3. Nein, ein kleines Glas. 4. Ein Bier, bitte. 5. Nein, ein großes Bier. 6. Nichts, danke.

3 1 1. Obst; 2. Pfund; 3. Brot; 4. Äpfel **2** 1. a); 2. b); 3. b); 4. a) **3** 1. Guten Morgen. 2. Ein Brot, bitte. 3. Haben Sie Äpfel? 4. Ein Pfund, bitte. 5. Was kostet das? 6. Sechs Mark – bitte. 7. Auf Wiedersehen.

4 1 1. a); 2. a); 3. b); 4. b); 5. a) **2** 1. a); 2. b) **3** 1. c); 2. b); 3. f); 4. d); 5. h); 6 g); 7. e); 8. a).

5 1 1. a); 2. b); 3. a); 4. a); 5. b); 6. b); 7. b) **2** 1. 3 sons; Kai, Tim, Andi; 4, 6, 10; 2. 2 daughters; 1 son; Susi, Anja, Frank; 2, 5, 7 **3** 1. d); 2. c); 3. a); 4. b).

6 1 1. b); 2. c); 3. d); 4. a) **2** 1. Dortmund; two; single; 13 Mark; 18.20; 16 2. Bremen; one; return; 17 Mark; 19.00; 11; **3** 6.; 4.; 2.; 5. then 7.; 3.; 1.; 8. or 1.; 8.; 7.; 3.

7 1 1. c); 2. b); 3. a); 4. b); 5. a) **2** 1. single; bath; 3; 3 2. 1 single, 1 double; shower; 1; 4, 9 **3** Guten Abend. 2. Haben Sie ein Zimmer frei? 3. Ein Doppelzimmer. 4. Mit Bad. 5. Für drei Nächte. 6. Für zwei Personen.

8 1 1. a); 2. b); 3. b); 4. b); 5. a); 6. b) **2** Frau Klein – Austrian; cinema, television, sports. Herr Williams – English; reading, travelling **3** 1. Ich komme aus London. Das ist in England. 2. Nein, ich bin Engländer(in). 3. Ja, mein Hobby ist Fernsehen. 4. Ich lese gern.

9 1 1. b); 2. a); 3. a); 4. b); 5. b) **2** true: 1.; 4.; 5.; false: 2.; 3.; 6. **3** 1. c); 2. e); 3. a); 4. b); 5. d); 6. f).

10 1 1. a); 2. b); 3. b); 4. b); 5. b) **2** Dortmund – cold; rainy. Munich – warm; good; windy **3** 1. Es ist sehr schön. Die Sonne scheint. 2. Nein, es ist nicht kalt. Es ist warm. 3. Ja, es regnet. 4. Das Wetter ist schlecht. Es ist sehr kalt.

11 1 1. a); 2. a); 3. b); 4. b) **2** a) toothache; b) tablets; c) three times a day; d) plasters; e) cold; f) 19 Marks **3** 1. Ja, ich bin erkältet. 2. Ja, ich habe Halsschmerzen. 3. Nein, mein Kopf tut weh. 4. Ja, meine Frau hat Zahnschmerzen. 5. Haben Sie Heftpflaster, bitte? 6. Was kostet das?

12 1 1. Montag; 2. Freitag; 3. Dienstag; 4. Donnerstag; 5. Sonntag; 6. Mittwoch **2** Monday: cinema; Tuesday: theatre; Thursday: restaurant with husband; Sunday 7 pm in town **3** 1. Nein, am Montag geht es nicht. 2. Nein, am Dienstag gehe ich ins Kino. 3. Nein, am Mittwoch gehen wir ins Restaurant. 4. Nein, am Donnerstag geht es nicht. 5. Nein, am Freitag gehen wir ins Theater. 6. Ja, am Sonnabend und Sonntag habe ich Zeit.

13 1 Ich bin Donna Miller. Ich wohne in London. Ich bin Engländerin. Mein Mann ist Amerikaner. **2** Herr Smith; San Francisco; America. Frau Klein; Luzern; Switzerland **3** 1. Mein

Name ist ... 2. Ich wohne in ... Das ist in ... 3. Und Sie? Kommen Sie aus Deutschland? 4. Ach, Sie sind Schweizerin. 5. Wo wohnen Sie in der Schweiz? 6. Ich kenne Bern gut. Bern ist eine schöne Stadt.

14 1 Bratwurst; Schnitzel; Gemüse; Mineralwasser; Pommes frites; Forelle; Kartoffelsalat 2 1. b); 2. a) 3 1. Zahlen, bitte! 2. Eine Bratwurst und Pommes frites. 3. Ein Schnitzel mit Kartoffelsalat. 4. Ein Bier und ein Mineralwasser. 5. Was macht das zusammen? 6. Hier – 70 Mark. Stimmt so!

15 1 1. a); 2. b); 3. a); 4. a); 5. a); 6. b) 2 1. a); 2. c) ; 3. b); 4.c) 3 1. Ich möchte eine Jeans. 2. Nein, diese Jeans ist zu teuer. 3. Nein, sie gefällt mir nicht. 4. Wo ist die Umkleidekabine, bitte? 5. Diese Jeans ist zu groß. 6. Diese Jeans passt.

16 1 1. d); 2. e); 3. c); 4. a); 5. b) 2 1. a); 2. b) 3 1. Entschuldigung! 2. Ich suche die Bank 3. Gehen Sie bis zur Kreuzung. 4. Nehmen Sie die erste Straße rechts. 5. Gehen Sie bis zur Ampel. 6. Nehmen Sie die zweite Straße links.

17 1 1. 3.15; 2. 6.30pm; 3. 2.19pm; 4. 8.50; 5. 7.30 2 1. Viertel vor sieben; 2. Siebzehn Uhr vierzig; 3. Halb elf; 4. Achtzehn Uhr sieben; 5. Viertel nach eins; 6. Fünfzehn Uhr dreißig 3 1. 19 Uhr 12; 2. Zehn nach neun; 3. 23 Uhr 58; 4. Fünf vor fünf. 5. Viertel vor sechs; 6. Halb acht.

18 1 1. Welcher Bus fährt zum Flughafen? 2. Wie komme ich zum Bahnhof? 3. Wo ist die nächste Bushaltestelle? 4. Welche U-Bahn fährt zum Bahnhof? 5. Kann ich Ihnen helfen? 2 true: 1.; 3; false: 2.; 4. 3 1.

Wie komme ich zum Bahnhof, bitte? 2. Wo ist die nächste U-Bahn-Station? 3. Welcher Bus fährt zum Flughafen? 4. Wo ist die nächste Bushaltestelle, bitte? 5. Welche U-Bahn fährt zum Flughafen? 6. Wie komme ich zum Theater?

19 1 2. vom achtzehnten bis zum neunzehnten Juni; 3. vom vierten bis zum achten Juli; 4. vom zweiundzwanzigsten bis zum dreiundzwanzigsten August 2 from 14 to 15 June; one night; single; with TV; with a shower; half board; 500 Schillings 3 1. Kann ich ein Zimmer reservieren? 2. Für vier Nächte, bitte. 3. Ein Doppelzimmer, bitte. 4. Nein, mit Dusche und Fernseher.

20 1 1. c); 2. a); 3. b); 4. c); 5. a); 6. c) 2 true: 2.; false: 1., 3., 4. 3 1. Meine Hobbys sind Musik und Fußball. 2. Ich gehe am liebsten ins Theater. 3. Ich gehe lieber ins Kino. 4. Was machen Sie am liebsten? 5. Haben Sie Hobbys? 6. Gehen Sie ins Kino?

21 1 1. Es gibt viele Sehenswürdigkeiten. 2. Ich wohne auf einem Bauernhof. 3. Was gibt es in Berlin zu sehen? 4. Fulham ist ein Stadtteil von London. 5. Ich komme aus Parching. 6. Es gibt zu viel Verkehr. 7. Lübeck ist eine schöne alte Stadt. 2 Erding; small town; south of Munich; yes, nice old town, very quiet; sights, theatre, cinema, shops 3 1. Ich wohne in Lübeck. 2. Nein, das ist eine kleine Stadt nördlich von Hamburg. 3. Nein, ich wohne auf einem Bauernhof. 4. Es gibt viele Sehenswürdigkeiten. Lübeck ist eine schöne alte Stadt.

22 1 1. a); 2. b); 3. b); 4. a) 2 south: hot and windy – 23 degrees; north: thunderstorm and hot – 22 degrees; west: cold and cloudy – 17 degrees; east: warm and rainy – 20 degrees **3** 2. Im Norden ist es wolkig. 19 Grad. 3. Im Osten gibt es ein Gewitter. 20 Grad. 4. Im Westen ist es wolkig und windig. 22 Grad. 5. Im Süden ist es heiß und windig. 25 Grad. 6. Im Norden regnet es. 18 Grad.

23 **1** 1. a); 2. a); 3. b); 4. b)
2 cold: sore throat, headache, cough; medicine; once a day; stay in bed and come back tomorrow **3** 1. Ich habe Bauchschmerzen 2. Ich habe Grippe. 3. Mein Kopf tut weh. 4. Ich habe Durchfall. 5. Ich habe Husten. 6. Mein Hals tut weh.

24 **1** 1. b); 2. b); 3. b); **2** 1. true: b); c); d); false: a) 2. true: a); b); c); false: d)
3 1. Ich gehe ins Kino. Was machen Sie heute Abend? 2. Was machen Sie morgen? 3. Am Sonnabend habe ich frei. Treffen wir uns? 4. Wollen wir ins Theater gehen? 5. In der Stadt. Wann treffen wir uns?

25 **1** 1. Darf ich vorstellen? 2. Ich muss mich beeilen. 3. Lass uns schwimmen gehen! 4. Ich möchte lieber ins Kino gehen. **2** 1. her friend Karin Hart; 2. to the opera 3. 7pm **3** 1 Lass uns in die Stadt gehen. 2. Ja, gut. Welcher Film läuft? 3. Der Film ist sehr lustig. 4. Ich muss mich beeilen – ich gehe ins Theater. 5. Die Vorstellung beginnt um halb neun.

26 **1** 1. a); 2. a); 3. b); 4. b) **2** cup of coffee with milk and no sugar, pot of tea with lemon; cheesecake without cream, apple strudel with cream
3 1. Ich möchte eine Tasse Kaffee mit Milch aber ohne Zucker. 2. Ein Kännchen Tee mit Zitrone und mit Zucker. 3. Eine Tasse Tee mit Zucker aber ohne Milch. 4. Ich möchte ein Stück Apfelstrudel mit Sahne. 5. Ein

Stück Schokoladentorte. 6. Nein, ein Stück Schokoladentorte ohne Sahne. 7. Ein Stück Käsekuchen mit Sahne, bitte.

27 **1** 1. b); 2. a); 3. a); 4. a); 5. b)
2 stationery: first floor; films: basement; gifts: second floor; magazines: ground floor **3** 1. Wo finde ich Bücher, bitte? 2. Entschuldigung. Ich suche Schreibwaren. 3. Wo finde ich Filme, bitte? 4. Wo ist die Geschenkabteilung, bitte? 5. Entschuldigung – wo finde ich Zeitschriften? 6. Wo ist die Rolltreppe, bitte?

28 **1** 1. Richtung; 2. Autobahn; 3. nächste; 4. zweihundert **2** true: 2.; 5.; false: 1.; 3.; 4. **3** 1. Entschuldigung! Wie komme ich zum Flughafen? 2. Wie weit ist es bis zum Flughafen? 3. Wie komme ich zur Autobahn 1? 4. Wie komme ich am besten nach Bremen? 5. Wo ist die nächste Tankstelle?

29 **1** 1. a); 2. b); 3. b); 4. b) **2** 1. green shirt: 36 Mark;. 2. blue dress: 42 Mark 30; 3. red T-Shirt: 21 Mark 50; total: 99 Mark 80; cash **3** 1. Das blaue Kleid kostet zweiundsiebzig Mark. 2. Das grüne T-Shirt kostet achtunddreißig Mark. 3. Das rote Hemd kostet zweiundvierzig Mark. 4. Die braunen Schuhe kosten neunundsechzig Mark und fünfzig Pfennig. 5. Die Jeans kostet fünfundachtzig Mark. 6. Das grüne Kleid kostet einundfünfzig Mark.

30 **1** 1. Was kostet eine Fahrkarte nach Hamburg? 2. Wo muss ich aussteigen? 3. Sie müssen in Hannover umsteigen. 4. Wo kaufe ich Fahrkarten? 5. Sie nehmen am besten die Linie 6. **2** 1. station; suburban train; yes 2. Dortmund – return, first class; 250 Marks **3** 1. Welcher Bus fährt zum

Bahnhof? 2. Wo muss ich aussteigen? 3. Wo kaufe ich Fahrkarten? 4. Was kostet eine Fahrkarte nach Berlin? 5. Muss ich umsteigen?

31 1 1. d); 2. c); 3. a); 4. b)
2 1. Hotel; 2. rufe; 3. Woche; 4. voll; 5. empfehlen; 6. sehr 3 1. Gibt es ein Hotel oder eine Pension hier in der Nähe? 2. Ja, für mich und meine Frau. 3. Nein, ein Doppelzimmer mit Bad und Fernseher. 4. Für eine Woche. 5. Dort sind keine Zimmer frei? 6. Können Sie ein anderes Hotel empfehlen?

32 1 1. Im Winter fahre ich Ski. 2. Am liebsten schwimme ich. 3. Ich jogge jeden Tag. 4. Mein anderes Hobby ist Schach. 5. Im Sommer spiele ich Tennis. 6. Ich koche jedes Wochenende. 2 true: 1.; 2.; false: 3.; 4.; 5. 3 1. Ja, mein Hobby ist Sport. 2. Im Sommer spiele ich Tennis, und ich jogge jeden Tag. 3. Im Winter mache ich Skilanglauf. 4. Ja, ich spiele gern Schach. Aber am liebsten koche ich. 5. Was machen Sie im Winter? 6. Ja, Bücher finde ich auch gut.

33 1 1. b)/d); 2. c); 3. e); 4. a); 5. b)/d) 2 Bremen for a week; sightseeing tour, walk through the centre of town; map, list of restaurants and hotels 3 1. Ja. Ich möchte die Stadt besichtigen. 2. Können Sie eine Stadtrundfahrt empfehlen? 3. Sieht man viele Sehenswürdigkeiten? 4. Haben Sie auch eine Broschüre über Berlin? 5. Haben Sie auch eine Liste von Hotels und Restaurants? 6. Ich möchte auch einen Stadtplan, bitte.

34 1 1. b); 2. c); 3. a); 4. b); 5. c); 6. a) 2 1. Was machen Sie im Herbst? 2. Was machen Sie im Frühling? 3. Was machen Sie in den Sommerferien? 4. Was machen Sie zu Ostern? 5. Was

machen Sie im Winter? 3 Dezember; Juni; Oktober; April; August.

35 1 1. wallet, 90 Marks 2. black bag, wallet and keys 3. camera, in town 2 1. d); 2. c); 3. b); 4. a) 3 1. meine Geldbörse; 2. und meine Schlüssel; 3. und mein Pass; 4. und mein Buch; 5. und meine Fahrkarte.

36 1 1. d); 2. c); 3. b); 4. a)
2 Bremen; for seven years; Hamburg; worked in a hotel; secretary; doctor
3 1. Ich wohne seit vier Jahren in Berlin. 2. Früher habe ich in Hamburg gewohnt. 3. Ich wohne seit zwei Jahren in Berlin. 4. Ich war dort in einem Hotel.

37 1 1 a); 2. b); 3. b); 4. a)
2 1. Jan Kaiser; male; four; small and slim, brown eyes, glasses, short red hair; 2. Franz Müller; male; 68; tall and quite fat, green eyes, bald, white moustache 3 1. Nein, er hat blaue Augen. 2. Nein, er hat eine Glatze. 3. Nein, er ist klein und dick.

38 1 1. b); 2. b); 3. a); 4. a); 5. b); 6. a) 2 1. meatball with french fries, mineral water, curried sausage with ketchup and mayonnaise; coke 3 1. Ich möchte eine Bratwurst mit Senf, bitte. 2. Eine Bockwurst mit Salat, bitte. 3. Eine kleine Bockwurst, bitte. 4. Eine Frikadelle mit Pommes frites und Ketschup. 5. Eine große Cola und einen Orangensaft, bitte.

39 1 1. a); 2. b); 3. a); 4. b) 2 true: 2.; 3.; 4.; false: 1 3 1. Nein, ich kaufe Wurst in der Metzgerei. 2. Nein, ich kaufe Gemüse in der Gemüsehandlung. 3. Nein, ich kaufe Brot in der Bäckerei. 4. Nein, ich kaufe Aufschnitt in der Metzgerei.

40 1 1. c); 2. d); 3. b); 4. a)
2 1. the supermarket; 2. right through

the pedestrian subway, left up to the lights, right over the bridge – supermarket is on the left – next to the pharmacy; 3. she doesn't know where it is
3 1. Sie gehen hier um die Ecke. 2. Sie gehen über die Brücke und dann rechts. 3. Sie gehen durch den Fußgängertunnel. 4. Sie gehen bis zur Ampel und dann geradeaus.

UNIT 41 **1** 1. a); 2. b); 3. b); 4. a); 5. a)
2 £200 – DM 461; £150 – FR 274
3 1. Ich möchte einen Reisescheck einlösen. 2. Ich möchte für 200 Pfund D-Mark. 3. Und ich möchte 150 Pfund in Schweizer Franken wechseln. 4. Ja. Ich möchte 250 Dollar in D-Mark wechseln. 5. Und ich möchte 300 Dollar in Schweizer Franken wechseln.

UNIT 42 **1** 1. b); 2. b); 3. b); 4. a) **2** Johann Ahlers; 46; lives in Vienna; sales assistant; centre of town (Glockenstraße); car in summmer – tube in winter; reading, tennis **3** 1. Ich bin Architekt von Beruf. 2. Ich arbeite in der Innenstadt. 3. Nein, ich fahre mit dem Bus zur Arbeit. 4. Die Fahrt dauert 30 Minuten.

UNIT 43 **1** 1. b); 2. a); 3. b); 4. a); 5 b)
2 room: second floor; lift: ground floor – on the left; telephone: ground floor – on the right; dining room: first floor
3 1. Ich habe zwei Zimmer reserviert. 2. Nein – ein Doppelzimmer für mich und meine Frau und ein Einzelzimmer für meine Tochter. 3. Nein, mit Balkon und Telefon. 4. Sind sie mit Blick auf die Berge? 5. Nein, mit Vollpension. Wo ist der Speiseraum, bitte? 6. Wann gibt es Frühstück und Abendessen?

UNIT 44 **1** 1. Freitag soll es schneien. 2. Morgen soll es Regen geben. 3. Übermorgen soll es sonnig sein. 4. Montag soll es ein Gewitter geben. 5. Morgen soll es windig sein. 6. Donnerstag soll es zu heiß sein. **2** 1. the weather is too bad – it's supposed to snow; 2. thunderstorm and rain; 3. Friday; 4. they are going into town
3 1. Nein, morgen soll es ein Gewitter geben. 2. Nein, übermorgen soll es Regen geben. 3. Nein, Montag soll es zu heiß sein. 4. Nein, Mittwoch soll es schneien. 5. Nein, Donnerstag soll es windig sein. 6. Ja, Freitag soll es sonnig sein.

UNIT 45 **1** 1. b); 2. a); 3. b); 4. b) **2** true: 1.; 3; 5.; false: 2.; 4.; 6. **3** 1. Was gibt es dort zu sehen? 2. Was können Sie noch empfehlen? 3. Kann man den Dom besichtigen? 4. Wann ist der Dom geöffnet? 5. Und wann ist er geschlossen?

UNIT 46 **2** America – Florida; summer: too hot, rain; winter: wet **3** 1. Guten Abend. Nein, ich komme aus England. 2. Wo wohnt Ihre Tochter denn? 3. Ich wohne in Newcastle. Das ist im Norden. 4. Ja, bei uns ist es im Winter immer sehr kalt!

UNIT 47 **1** 1. b); 2. a); 3. a); 4. b) **2** 1. Ich habe eine Panne. 2. Der Motor ist kaputt. 3. Ich habe eine Reifenpanne. 4. Die Scheinwerfer sind kaputt. 5. Ich habe kein Benzin. **3** 1. Ich habe eine Panne. 2. Nein, der Motor ist nicht kaputt. Ich habe kein Benzin. 3. Ja, und die Scheinwerfer sind auch kaputt. 4. Nicht weit von Pinneberg in Richtung Hamburg. 5. Nein. Ich bin auf der Autobahn 1. 6. In der Nähe der Autobahnabfahrt. 7. Ja. Können Sie helfen?

UNIT 48 **1** 1. Morgen abend gehe ich mit meiner Frau aus. 2. Morgen früh fahre ich in die Stadt. 3. Morgen nachmittag mache ich einen Ausflug. **2** 1. c); a); b); 2. b); c); a) **3** 1. Morgen früh mache ich einen Ausflug. 2. Nein, ich mache eine

Wanderung an den See. 3. Morgen nachmittag gehe ich in die Stadt. 4. Nein. Ich gehe ins Museum. Und ich will Andenken kaufen. 5. Morgen abend gehe ich mit meiner Frau aus – wir wollen essen gehen.

49 **1** 1. c); 2. a); 3. d); 4. b); **2** Name; alt; Brüder; Schwester; Eltern; veheiratet; geschieden; keine; Hund; Katze **3** 1. Nein, ich bin verheiratet. Sind Sie verheiratet? 2. Ja, ich habe einen Sohn. Er ist sechs Jahre alt. 3. Ja. Meine Tochter ist 13 Jahre alt. 4. Ja, ich habe einen Bruder. Er wohnt in Berlin. 5. Meine Eltern wohnen in Hamburg.

50 **1** 1. b); 2. a); 3. c) **2** fried egg with bacon; boiled egg; muesli; rolls with ham and cheese; rolls with jam and honey **3** 1. ein gekochtes Ei; 2. Toast mit Honig; 3. Müsli mit Milch; 4. zwei Brötchen mit Aufschnitt; 5. eine Tasse Kaffee.

51 **1** 5.; 1.; 4.; 2.; 6.; 3. **2** true: 1.; 2.; 5.; false: 3.; 4. **3** 1. Guten Tag, ich suche einen Mantel. 2. Größe 40, bitte. 3. Nein, die Farbe gefällt mir nicht. 4. Nein, er ist zu bunt – haben Sie den Mantel auch in Schwarz? 5. Nein, er ist zu klein. Haben Sie den Mantel eine Nummer größer? 6. Nein, dieser Mantel ist zu kurz.

52 **1** 1. Wald; 2. Fuß; 3. Schloss; 4. Jugendherberge; 5. Freibad; 6. Drogerie **2** true: 1.; 3.; 5.; false: 2.; 4; 6. **3** 1. Entschuldigen Sie – ich bin fremd hier. 2. Wie komme ich am besten zur Jugendherberge? 3. Ich bin zu Fuß – ist es weit? 4. Wo ist das Schwimmbad? 5. Und wo ist das Schloss? 6. Wo ist die nächste Drogerie?

53 **1** 1. c); 2. a)/d); 3. b); 4. e); 5. a)

2 Name; Viertel; möchte; sprechen; Telefonnummer; Meine; Widerhören **3** 1. Ja, bitte. Meine Telefonnummer ist 0360 67 03 24. 2. Meine Faxnummer ist 0360 44 77 58. 3. Ich habe noch eine Frage: Wie ist Ihre Faxnummer, bitte? 4. 0531 69 82 74. Vielen Dank – auf Wiederhören!

54 **1** 10.; 3.; 5.; 7.; 2.; 8.; 4.; 9.; 1., 6. **2** Hamburg; first class; return; 286 Mark, 316 Mark; non-smoking; window seat **3** 1. f); 2. d); 3. a); 4. c); 5. b); 6. e).

55 **1** 1. b)/c)/e); 2. d); 3. a)/b)/e); 4. f); 5. a); 6. b)/c)/e) **2** 1. a); 2. b); 3. a); 4. b) **3** 1. Haben Sie einen Platz für drei Nächte? 2. Nein, für einen Wohnwagen. 3. Für drei Personen. 4. Gibt es einen Spielraum? 5. Gibt es auch eine Waschmaschine?

56 **1** true: 4.; 5.; 6.; false: 1.; 2.; 3. **2** boattrips: 15 May; 15 September; 45 minutes; every hour; from 10.30am to 5.30pm; 7 Marks; 4 Marks 50; boat hire – rowing boat: two: 11 Marks per hour; four: 15 Marks per hour; pedal boat: two; 9 Marks per hour **3** 1. 29 Mark; 2. 25 Mark; 3. 37 Mark.

57 **1** 1. Wann kommen Sie in Berlin an? 2. Ich freue mich schon sehr auf Ihren Besuch. 3. Sie können bei uns übernachten. 4. Kommen Sie mit dem Flugzeug? 5. Wir müssen am 5. Mai wieder zurück. **2** 1. Munich; 2. July; 3. to let them stay with them; 4. 7 July – 9 July; 5. by train; 6. station **3** 1. Können wir uns treffen? 2. Haben Sie Platz für uns? 3. Wir kommen mit dem Zug. 4. Ich freue mich schon sehr!

58 **1** 1. Knoblauch; Knoblauch; 2. Aspirin; 3. Milch, Milch; 4. Hausstaub **2** true: 1.; 4.; false: 2.; 3.; 5.; 6. **3** 1.

Furchtbar! Es ist nass und kalt. 2. Nein, es ist nicht windig. Und wie ist das Wetter in Hamburg? 3. Oh nein, ich habe nämlich Heuschnupfen. 4. Ja, ich bin allergisch gegen Pollen und Katzen.

59 **1** 1. b); 2. a)/c); 3. d); 4. a)/c)
2 1. head hurts, right leg is broken; ambulance; 2. cyclist; left leg hurts, back hurts; ambulance; 3. husband; heart attack; police, ambulance
3 1. Sind Sie verletzt? 2. Schnell – rufen Sie einen Krankenwagen!
3. Bewegen Sie sich nicht! 4. Mein linker Arm tut weh! 5. Mein rechtes Bein ist gebrochen! 6. Mein Rücken tut weh!

60 **1** 1. c); 2. d); 3. a); 4. b)
2 1. c); 2. d); 3. a)/b); 4. e); 5. a)/b)
3 1. Guten Abend, Herr Berger. Haben Sie heute Abend Zeit? 2. Ich möchte Sie gern zum Essen einladen. 3. Wo möchten Sie essen gehen? 4. Nein, ich esse kein Fleisch. Ich bin Vegetarier. 5. Nein, es tut mir leid – türkische Küche mag ich nicht. 6. Nein, chinesisch esse ich nicht so gern. 7. Ja, dort gibt es auch vegetarische Gerichte.

Grammar Summary

Nouns

A noun is a person, a thing or a place. German nouns always begin with a capital letter. There are three groups of nouns: (masculine, feminine and neuter), and nouns can either be singular (one) or plural (more than one).

Plural nouns

German plural nouns vary a lot – there are no easy rules. It's therefore best to learn each noun with its plural.

Articles

These are the words for 'a/the' that go in front of a noun, and they depend on whether the noun they go with is masculine, feminine or neuter:

	the	a
masculine	*der* **Mann**	*ein* **Mann**
feminine	*die* **Frau**	*eine* **Frau**
neuter	*das* **Kind**	*ein* **Kind**

The plural of **der/die/das** is always **die**.

Pronouns

Pronouns are small words like 'I', 'you', 'he' which can replace nouns.

I	**ich**	you	**ihr**
you	**du**	they	**sie**
he/she/it	**er/sie/es**	you	**Sie**
we	**wir**		

Sie and *du*

Sie is the polite or formal form of 'you' and is used to talk to strangers, to aquaintances, to other people one doesn't know very well and to colleagues.

The informal **du** is only used for family, children, friends and animals.

Verbs

A verb is a 'doing' word which describes an action or a state. The ends of verbs change according to who is doing the action. Most verb endings follow a regular pattern:

ich	**trinke**	I drink
du	**trinkst**	you drink (*informal*)
er/sie/es	**trinkt**	he/she/it drinks
wir	**trinken**	we drink
ihr	**trinkt**	you drink
sie	**trinken**	they drink
Sie	**trinken**	you drink (*polite*)

In dictionaries, verbs are always listed with their infinitive (the 'to ...' form of the verb). German infinitives always end with **-n** or **-en**: **trinken** (to drink) .

Sein and haben

Irregular verbs don't follow that pattern. The most important irregular verbs to know are **sein** (to be) and **haben** (to have):

	sein			haben	
ich	*bin*	I am	ich	ha*be*	I have
du	*bist*	you are	du	ha*st*	you have
er/sie/es	*ist*	he/she/it is	er/sie/es	ha*t*	he/she/it has
wir	*sind*	we are	wir	hab*en*	we have
ihr	*seid*	you are	ihr	hab*t*	you have
sie	*sind*	they are	sie	hab*en*	they have
Sie	*sind*	you are	Sie	hab*en*	you have

Modal verbs

Modal verbs add meaning to another verb in the sentence. When using modal verbs, the second verb in the sentence takes the infinitive and goes to the end of the sentence:

Ich arbeite.	I work.
Ich *muß* **arbeit***en***.**	I have to work.

Here are the forms of all the modal verbs you need to know:

	können	könnte	müssen	sollen	wollen
	can	could	must	should	want to
ich	kann	könnte	muss	soll	will
du	kannst	könntest	musst	sollst	willst
er/sie/es	kann	könnte	muss	soll	will
wir	können	könnten	müssen	sollen	wollen
ihr	könnt	könntet	müsst	sollt	wollt
sie	können	könnten	müssen	sollen	wollen
Sie	können	könnten	müssen	sollen	wollen

Tenses

The past tense

The past tense is used to describe something that has happened in the past. It is usually formed with the verb **haben** (to have). When using the past tense with **haben**, the second verb (the past participle) changes its form and goes to the end of the sentence:

Ich *kaufe* ein Geschenk.	Ich habe ein Geschenk *gekauft*.
Sie *findet* die Tasche.	Sie hat die Tasche *gefunden*.

Verbs which end in **-ieren** do not need the **ge-** in their past participle form:

telefonieren	→	**Ich habe telefoniert.**

Future tense

You can talk about the future by simply using the present tense and a time expression:

Am Sonntag gehe ich ins Kino.	On Sunday I am going to the cinema.

Adjectives

Adjectives (words like **groß** – large) describe a noun. When they go with an article in front of a noun, the adjective and the article change their endings depending on whether the noun is masculine, feminine or neuter and how the noun functions in the sentence. Here are the rules:

der/ein Mann	Dort ist *der* groß*e/ein* groß*er* Mann.	There is the/a tall man.
die/eine Frau	Dort ist *die/eine* jung*e* Frau.	There is the/a young woman.
das/ein Haus	Dort ist *das* alt*e/ein* alt*es* Haus.	There is the/an old house.

The noun in these sentences is the person or thing doing something – it is the subject of the sentence. In the following sentences the noun has something done to it – it is the object of the sentence. (The subject of the sentence is **ich**.)

der/ein Mann	Ich sehe *den/einen* groß*en* Mann.	I see the/a tall man.
die/eine Frau	Ich sehe *die/eine* jung*e* Frau.	I see the/a young woman.
das/ein Haus	Ich sehe *das* alt*e/ein* alt*es* Haus.	I see the/a old house.

Making comparisons

This is how adjectives change in their comparative form:

klein	small	**klein*er***	smaller
alt	old	***ä*lt*er***	older
groß	big	**gr*öß*er**	bigger

Some comparative forms are irregular:

gut	good	**besser**	better	**am besten**	best

Possessive adjectives

The rules for **mein/Ihr** (my/your) are almost the same as for **ein/eine**.

a	ein	Mann	eine	Frau	ein	Kind
my	mein	Mann	meine	Frau	mein	Kind
your	Ihr	Mann	Ihr	Mann	Ihr	Kind

Prepositions

Prepositions are words like 'in', 'at' and 'on'. They stand in front of a noun and link it to the sentence. The articles take different endings depending on the preposition and on whether the noun they go with is masculine, feminine or neuter.

durch (through), **für** (for), **um** (around):

der Bahnhof	→	durch *den* Bahnhof
die Stadt	→	durch *die* Stadt
das Haus	→	durch *das* Haus

von (from, of), **zu** (to):

der Bahnhof	→	von *dem* Bahnhof
die Stadt	→	von *der* Stadt
das Haus	→	von *dem* Haus

an, auf, hinter, in, neben, über, vor can take either of those endings: if they indicate movement (i.e. if used with verbs like **gehen,** to go) they follow the rules for **durch**. If used with verbs which show where something is (e.g. **wohnen** to live) they follow the rules for **von**.

Note these shortened forms:

| an dem | → | *am* | in dem | → | *im* |
| an das | → | *ans* | in das | → | *ins* |

Questions

Questions which only need **ja** or **nein** as an answer are formed like this:

Wir gehen in die Stadt. → **Gehen wir in die Stadt?** Are we going into town?

To get more information, a question word is added at the beginning of the question:

Wann **gehen wir in die Stadt?** When are we going into town?

wann?	when?	**wie lange?**	how long?
was?	what?	**wo?**	where?
welche/r/s?	which?	**woher?**	where from?
wie?	how?	**wohin?**	where to?
wieviel?	how much?	**seit wann?**	since when?/for how long?

Word order

Commands

For commands or instructions the verb is put at the beginning of the sentence:

Sie gehen links.	→	***Gehen* Sie links!**

Expressions of time

When an expression of time comes first in a sentence, the verb follows directly before the subject:

Am Wochenende	**gehe**	**ich**	**in die Stadt.**
expression of time	*verb*	*subject*	

Time – manner – place

In sentences with several elements, the rules are as follows:

Ich fahre	**am Wochenende**	**mit dem Zug**	**nach Hamburg.**
	time	*manner*	*place*

Negation

If you only want to negate one particular word, the word **nicht** (not) goes in front of this word:

Ich gehe ins Kino.	**Ich gehe *nicht* ins Kino.**

If you want to negate a whole sentence or phrase, the **nicht** goes at the end of that sentence/phrase:

Ich mag Kuchen.	**Ich mag Kuchen *nicht*.**
Kuchen mag ich.	**Kuchen mag ich *nicht*.**

Vocabulary

This list contains the most important German words from the course. The plural of nouns appears in brackets, as follows:

Abend(e)	add **e: Abende**
Abendessen(–)	plural unchanged: **Abendessen**
Adresse(n)	add **n: Adressen**
Amerikanerin(nen)	add **nen: Amerikanerinnen**
Apfel (¨)	stem vowel becomes an umlaut: **Äpfel**
Architekt(en)	add **en: Architekten**
Ausflug(¨e)	add **e** and stem vowel becomes an umlaut: **Ausflüge**
Auto(s)	add **s: Autos**
Buch(¨er)	add **er** and stem vowel becomes an umlaut: **Bücher**
Deutscher(Deutsche)	irregular plural

If the noun appears without a plural form in brackets, either the plural isn't used very often, or no plural exists: **Altstadt**. If a word is followed by *pl.*, it is only used in the plural: **Bauchschmerzen**.

The gender of nouns is given as follows:

m. = masculine
f. = feminine
n. = neuter

A

Abend(e) *m.* evening
Abendessen(–) *n.* dinner
abends in the evening
abholen to pick up
Adresse(n) *f.* address
alles everything/all
also that is
alt old
Altstadt *f.* old town
am besten best
am liebsten best
Amerika United States
Amerikaner(–) *m.* American (man)
Amerikanerin(nen) *f.* American (woman)
Ampel(n) *f.* traffic lights
Andenken(–) *n.* souvenir
andere(r/s) other/another
angenehm delighted (to meet you)
ankommen to arrive
Anmeldeformular(e) *n.* registration form
Anmeldung *f.* reception
anprobieren to try on
anrufen to call
Apfel(¨) *m.* apple
Apotheke(n) *f.* chemist (shop)
Apotheker(–) *m.* chemist (male)
Apparat(e) *m.* receiver
arbeiten to work
ärgerlich annoying

Arm(e) *m.* arm
Ärztin(nen) *f.* doctor (female)
auch too
auf on
Aufschnitt *m.* cold meats
Auge(n) *n.* eye
aus from
Ausflug(¨e) *m.* excursion
ausgehen to go out
ausruhen to have a rest
aussehen to look like
aussteigen to get off
Ausweis(e) *m.* identification, passport
Auto(s) *n.* car
Autobahn(en) *f.* motorway

B

Bäckerei(en) *f.* bakery
Bad(¨er) *n.* bath(room)
Badezimmer(–) *n.* bathroom
Bahnhof(¨e) *m.* station
Balkon(s) *m.* balcony
Bank(en) *f.* bank
bar cash
Bauchschmerzen *pl.* stomach ache
Bauernhof(¨e) *m.* farm house
beeilen to hurry
beginnen to begin/start
Bein(e) *n.* leg
bekommen to get

Benzin *n.*   petrol
Berg(e) *m.*   mountain
Beruf(e) *m.*   profession
berühmt   famous
besichtigen   to visit/to have a look at
Besuch(e) *m.*   visit
Bett(en) *n.*   bed
bewegen   to move
bezahlen   to pay
Bier *n.*   beer
bis   as far as/up to
bitte   please
blau   blue
bleiben   to stay
Blick *m.*   view
Bockwurst(ˉe) *f.*   cooked sausage
Boot(e) *n.*   boat
Bratwurst(ˉe) *f.*   fried sausage
brauchen   to need
braun   brown
Briefmarke(n) *f.*   stamp
Brille(n) *f.*   glasses
Brot(e) *n.*   bread
Brötchen(–) *n.*   bread rolls
Brücke(n) *f.*   bridge
Bruder(ˉ) *m.*   brother
Buch(ˉer) *n.*   book
bunt   colourful
Büro(s) *n.*   office
Bus(se) *m.*   bus
Bushaltestelle(n) *f.*   bus stop

C **Campingplatz(ˉe)** *m.*   camp site
Currywurst(ˉe) *f.*   fried sausage with curry sauce

D **da**   there
danke   thank you
dann   then
dauern   to last
dazu   with that
denn   then
deutsch   German
Deutsche(–) *f.*   German (woman)
Deutscher(Deutsche) *m.*   German (man)
Deutschland *n.*   Germany
dick   fat
diese(r/s)   this
direkt   straight through
Dom *m.*   cathedral
Doppelzimmer(–) *n.*   double room
Dorf(ˉer) *n.*   village
dort   there
dreimal   three times
drin   in
dritte/r/s   third
Drogerie(en) *f.*   chemist (shop)
drüben   over there
durch   through
Durchfall *m.*   diarrhoea

dürfen   to be allowed to
Dusche(n) *f.*   shower

E

Ecke(n) *f.*   corner
Ei(er) *n.*   egg
ein/e   a
einfach   single
einkaufen   to go shopping
einladen   to invite
einlösen   to cash
einmal   once
Einzelzimmer(–) *n.*   single room
Eltern *pl.*   parents
empfehlen   to recommend
England   England
Engländer(–) *m.*   English man
Engländerin(nen) *f.*   English woman
Entschuldigung!   excuse me!
Erdgeschoss *n.*   ground floor
erkältet sein   to have a cold
erste/r/s   first
es   it
essen   to eat
etwas   something

F

fahren   to drive
Fahrkarte(n) *f.*   ticket
Fahrkartenschalter(–) *m.*   ticket office
Fahrrad(ˉer) *n.*   bicycle
Fahrstuhl(ˉe) *m.*   lift
Fahrt(en) *f.*   journey
Familie(n) *f.*   family
Farbe(n) *f.*   colour
Fensterplatz(ˉe) *m.*   window seat
Fernseher(–) *m.*   television (set)
Film(e) *m.*   film
finden   to find
Firma(Firmen) *f.*   company
fit   fit
Fleisch *n.*   meat
Flughafen(ˉ) *m.*   airport
Flugzeug(e) *n.*   plane
Forelle(n) *f.*   trout
Foto(s) *n.*   photo
fotografieren   to photograph
Frage(n) *f.*   question
Franken (–) *m.*   Franc
Frau(en) *f.*   Mrs, woman
frei   free, vacant
Freibad(ˉer) *n.*   open-air swimmig pool
fremd   foreign
freuen   to look forward to
Freund(e) *m.*   boyfriend/male friend
Freundin(nen) *f.*   girlfriend/female friend
Frikadelle(n) *f.*   meatball
früher   earlier
Frühling *m.*   spring
Frühstück *n.*   breakfast
Fundbüro(s) *n.*   lost property office
für   for

furchtbar awful
Fuß(¨sse) *m.* foot
Fußball(¨e) *m.* football
Fußgängertunnel(–) *m.* pedestrian subway

G **ganz** all
Garten(¨) *m.* garden
geben to give
gebrochen broken
gefallen to like
gegen to/against
gehen to go
gekocht boiled
Geld *n.* money
Geldbörse(n) *f.* wallet
Gemüse *n.* vegetables
Gemüsehandlung(en) *f.* greengrocer's
genau exactly
geöffnet open
geradeaus straight on
Gericht(e) *n.* food/dish
gern well
gern geschehen! you're welcome!
Geschäft(e) *n.* shop
geschehen to happen
Geschenk(e) *n.* gift
geschieden divorced
geschlossen closed
Geschwister *pl.* brothers and sisters
Gewitter(–) *n.* thunderstorm
Glas(¨er) *n.* glass
Glatze(n) *f.* bald head
gleich just
Gleis(e) *n.* platform
Grad *m.* degree
grau grey
Griechenland *n.* Greece
Grippe *f.* flu
groß large, tall
Größe(n) *f.* size
grün green
gut well

H **Haar(e)** *n.* hair
haben to have
Hähnchen(–) *n.* grilled chicken
halb half
Halbpension *f.* half board
Halsschmerzen *pl.* sore throat
Heftplaster(–) *n.* plaster
heiß hot
heißen to be called
helfen to help
Hemd(en) *n.* shirt
Herbst *m.* autumn
Herr(en) *m.* Mr
heute today
hier there/here
hin to
hinter behind

Hobby(s) *n.* hobby
hoch up
Honig *m.* honey
Hotel(s) *n.* hotel
Hund(e) *m.* dog
Husten *m.* cough

I **ich** I
Ihnen (to) you (polite)
Ihr/e your (polite)
immer always
in in
Innenstadt *f.* town centre
Insel(n) *f.* island
interessant interesting
interessieren to be interested

J **ja** yes
Jahr(e) *n.* year
Jeans(–) *f.* pair of jeans
jeder each
jetzt now
joggen to jog
Jugendherberge(n) *f.* youth hostel

K **Kaffee** *m.* coffee
Kakao *m.* chocolate (drink)
kalt cold
Kännchen(–) *n.* pot
kaputt broken
Karte(n) *f.* card
Kartoffelsalat *m.* potato salad
Käsekuchen *m.* cheesecake
Kasse(n) *f.* till
Katze(n) *f.* cat
kaufen to buy
Kaufhaus(¨er) *n.* department store
kein/e none
Kellner(–) *m.* waiter
kennen to know
Kilometer(–) *m.* kilometre
Kind(er) *n.* child
Kinderermäßigung(en) *f.* concession for children
Kino(s) *n.* cinema
Kirche(n) *f.* church
Klasse(n) *f.* class
Kleid(er) *n.* dress
klein small
kochen to cook
kommen to come
können could
Kopf(¨e) *m.* head
Kopfschmerzen *pl.* headache
kosten to cost
Krankenhaus(¨er) *n.* hospital
Krankenwagen(–) *m.* ambulance
Kreditkarte(n) *f.* credit card
Kreuzung(en) *f.* crossroads
Küche(n) *f.* kitchen/cuisine

Kunde(n) *m.* customer (male)
Kundin(nen) *f.* customer (female)
Kunst *f.* arts
kurz short

L
Land("er) *n.* country/countryside
lang long
langsam slow
lassen to let
laufen to run/to be shown
Lebensmittel *pl.* groceries
ledig single
leid tun to be sorry
leihen to hire
lesen to read
letzte/r/s last
lieber better
lila purple
Linie(n) *f.* line (of tram etc.)
links left
Liste(n) *f.* list
lockig curly
lustig funny

M
machen to do/to add up to
Malen *n.* painting
manchmal sometimes
Mantel(") *m.* coat
Mark(–) *f.* mark
Marmelade(n) *f.* jam
Majonäse *f.* mayonnaise
Medizin *f.* medicine
mein/e my
meinen to mean
meistens most of the time
Meter(–) *m.* metre
Metzgerei(en) *f.* butcher's
mich me
Milch *f.* milk
Mineralwasser *n.* mineral water
Minute(n) *f.* minute
mir me
mit by/with
mitkommen to come (along)
möchten would like
modern fashionable
mögen to like
Moment *m.* moment
Monat(e) *m.* month
morgen tomorrow
Morgen *m.* morning
Museum(Museen) *n.* museum
Musik *f.* music
Müsli *n.* muesli
müssen to have to

N
nach to/after/past
Nachmittag(e) *m.* afternoon
nachmittags in the afternoon
nächste/r/s nearest/next

Nacht("e) *f.* night
Nähe *f.* proximity
Name(n) *m.* name
nass wet
neben next
neblig foggy
nehmen to take
nett nice
nicht not
nicht wahr? isn't it?
Nichtraucher non-smoking (seat)
nichts nothing
noch still
Norden *m.* north
Nordsee *f.* North Sea
null zero
Nummer(n) *f.* number/size
nur only

O
Ober(–) *m.* waiter
Obst *n.* fruit
oder or
oft often
ohne without
Orangensaft *m.* orange juice
Osten *m.* east
Ostern *n.* Easter
Österreich *n.* Austria

P
Panne(n) *f.* breakdown
Park(s) *m.* park
Parkplatz("e) *m.* car park
Pass("e) *m.* passport
passen to fit
passieren to happen
Person(en) *f.* person
Pfennig(e) *m.* pence
Pferd(e) *n.* horse
Pfund(e) *n.* pound
Platz("e) *m.* space
Polizei *f.* police
Pommes frites *pl.* French fries
Post *f.* post office
Postkarte(n) *f.* postcard
praktisch convenient
Problem(e) *n.* problem

Q
Querstraße(n) *f.* cross roads

R
Radfahrer(–) *m.* cyclist
Raucher smoking (seat)
rechts right
Regen *m.* rain
regnen to rain
Reisen *n.* travelling
Reisescheck(s) *m.* traveller's cheque
reservieren to book
Restaurant(s) *n.* restaurant
Rezept(e) *n.* prescription
Richtung(en) *f.* direction

Rock("e) *m.* skirt
Rolltreppe(n) *f.* escalator
rot red
Rücken(–) *m.* back
Ruderboot(e) *n.* rowing boat
rufen to call
ruhig quiet

S sagen to say
Sahne *f.* cream
Salat(e) *m.* salat
S-Bahn(en) *f.* suburban train
Schach *n.* chess
Scheck(s) *m.* cheque
Scheinwerfer(–) *m.* headlight
Schiffsfahrt(en) *f.* boat trip
Schinken *m.* ham
schlank slim
schlecht bad
Schloss("er) *n.* palace/castle
Schlüssel(–) *m.* key
Schnee *m.* snow
schneien to snow
schnell quickly
Schnitzel(–) *n.* veal escalope
Schokoladentorte(n) *f.* chocolate gateau
schön beautiful
Schottland Scotland
Schreibwaren *pl.* stationery
Schuh(e) *m.* shoe
schwarz black
Schweiz *f.* Switzerland
Schweizer(–) *m.* Swiss (man)
Schweizerin(nen) *f.* Swiss (woman)
Schwester(n) *f.* sister
schwimmen to swim
seit since
See(n) *m.* lake
sehen to see
Sehenswürdigkeiten *pl.* sights
sehr very
sein to be
seit since
Seite(n) *f.* side
Sekretärin(nen) *f.* secretary
Senf *m.* mustard
sie they
Sie you (polite)
Ski *m.* ski
Skifahren *n.* skiing
Skilanglauf *m.* cross-country skiing
so so
sofort immediately
Sohn("e) *m.* son
sollen shall
Sommer *m.* summer
Sommerferien *pl.* summer break/holidays
Sonderangebot(e) *n.* special offer
Sonne *f.* sun
sonnig sunny

sonst else/otherwise
spät late
Spaziergang("e) *m.* stroll
Speck *m.* bacon
Speiseraum("e) *m.* dining room
Spiegelei(er) *n.* fried egg
spielen to play
Spielraum("e) *m.* games room
Stadt("e) *f.* town
Stadtplan("e) *m.* map
Stadtrundfahrt(en) *f.* sightseeing tour
Stadtteil(e) *m.* part of town
stark severe
Steakhaus("er) *n.* steak house
stimmen to be right
stimmt so! keep the change!
Stock *m.* floor
Straße(n) *f.* street
Stück(e) *n.* piece (of)
Stunde(n) *f.* hour
suchen to look for
Süden *m.* south
Supermarkt("e) *m.* supermarket
Süßwaren *pl.* confectionery
sympathisch nice/kind

T Tablette(n) *f.* tablet
Tag(e) *m.* day
Tankstelle(n) *f.* petrol station
tanzen to dance
Tasche(n) *f.* bag
Tasse(n) *f.* cup
tauschen to change
Tee *m.* tea
Telefon(e) *n.* telephone
Telefonzelle(n) *f.* phone box
Tennis *n.* tennis
teuer expensive
Theater(–) *n.* theatre
Toast *m.* toast
Tochter(") *f.* daughter
Tomate(n) *f.* tomato
tragen to wear
treffen to meet
trinken to drink
tun to do

U U-Bahn(en) *f.* tube/underground
U-Bahn-Station(en) *f.* tube/underground
station
über over/above/about/on/more than
übermorgen the day after tomorrow
übernachten to stay overnight
Übernachtung(en) *f.* overnight stay
Uhr(en) *f.* clock/watch
um at/around
Umkleidekabine(n) *f.* changing room
umsteigen to change
und and
Unfall("e) *m.* accident

ungefähr approximately
uns us
Untergeschoss *n.* basement
unterschreiben to sign

V

Vegetarier(–) *m.* vegetarian
vegetarisch vegetarian
verbinden to connect/put through
verheiratet married
verkaufen to sell
Verkäufer(–) *m.* shop assistant (male)
Verkäuferin(nen) *f.* shop assistant
(female)
Verkehr *m.* traffic
verletzt hurt
verlieren to lose
verreisen to go on holiday
verstehen to understand
viel much/many/a lot
vielleicht maybe
Viertel(–) *n.* quarter
voll full
Vollpension *f.* full board
von by/from/of
vor to/in front/before
vorstellen to introduce
Vorstellung(en) *f.* show

W

Wald(¨er) *m.* forest
wandern to hike
Wanderung(en) *f.* walk
wann when
warm warm
warten to wait
warum why
was what
was ist los? what's the problem?
Waschmaschine(n) *f.* washing machine
Waschraum(¨e) *m.* wash room
Wasser *n.* water
wehtun to hurt
Wein(e) *m.* wine
weiß white

weit far
welche/r/s which
Westen *m.* west
Wetter *n.* weather
Wettervorhersage(n) *f.* weather forecast
wie how
wieviel/wie viel(e) how much/many
wieder again
(auf) Wiedersehen good bye
wieso why
windig windy
Winter *m.* winter
wissen to know
wo where
Woche(n) *f.* week
woher where from
wohnen to live
Wohnung(en) *f.* flat
Wohnwagen(–) *m.* caravan
wolkig cloudy
wollen to want to

zahlen to pay
Zahnschmerzen *pl.* toothache
zeigen to show
Zeit f. time
Zeitschrift(en) *f.* magazine
Zelt(e) *n.* tent
Zimmer(–) *n.* room
Zitrone (n) *f.* lemon
zu to
zu/m/r to (the)
Zucker *m.* sugar
Zug(¨e) *m.* train
zumachen to close
zurück back, return
zurückfahren to go back
zurückrufen to call back
zusammen together
zuviel too much
zweimal twice
zweite/r/s second

Z

Grammar and Subject Indexes

Numbers refer to units

GRAMMAR

Adjectives:
  Endings 9, 29
  gern, lieber, am liebsten
    20
  Making comparisons 15
  Possessive adjectives 5, 7
Articles:
  der, die, das 4
  ein, eine, ein 7
  Plural 27
Cases:
  Accusative 33
Nouns:
  Compound nouns 6, 55
  Gender 4, 7, 60
  Nationalities 8
  Plurals 3, 27, 49, 55
  Professions 36
Numbers:
  1–10 5
  11–20 6
  20+ 14
  100+ 28, 41
  erste, ... dreißigste 19
  Telling the time 17
  zweimal, dreimal, ... 38
Prepositions:
  an 40
  auf 21, 40
  durch 40
  für 50
  gegen 58
  hinter 40
  in 13, 22, 40
  neben, **über**, **um** 40
  von 54
  vor, **zu** 40

Pronouns:
  du, Sie 2, 39
  mein, Ihr 5, 50
Questions:
  Formation 24
  Question words 18, 42, 56
Tenses:
  Future (present tense +
    time) 12
  Past tense with **haben** 35,
    43
Verbs:
  Endings 11
  gefallen 15, 51
  haben 11, 37, 46
  Infinitives 30, 32
  Irregular verbs 26
  Modal verbs:
    können 45, 47
    könnte 53
    müssen 30, 47
    sollen 31, 47
    wollen 44, 47
  sein 5, 37
  Regular verbs 23
Word order:
  Commands 16, 59
  Directions 52
  Expressions of time 12, 32
  Negation 25
  Questions 42
  Time–manner–place 34

SUBJECTS

Accidents and emergencies
  59
Accommodation 7, 9, 19, 31,
43, 55
Café, restaurant 2, 12, 14, 26,
  38, 50, 60
Camping 55
Countries, regions, towns and
  villages 13, 21, 33, 45, 57
Directions 4, 16, 28, 40, 52
Family 5, 49
Germany 13
Greetings 1, 5, 12
Health 11, 23
Hobbies and pastimes 8, 20,
  24, 25, 32, 44, 48, 56
Holidays 34
Hotels 7, 19, 31, 43, 50
Jobs 36
Lost property 35
Meeting up with friends 12,
  24, 44, 57
Money and payment 14, 29, 41
Motoring (breakdown) 47
Nationality 8
Numbers 5, 6, 28, 41
Shopping
  Clothes 15, 51
  Department store 27
  Food 3, 39
  Opening hours 15
Sightseeing 33, 45
Staying with friends 57
Telephone 53
Time of day 17
Travel
  Car 28
  Public transport 18, 30, 42,
  54
  Train 6, 54
Weather 10, 22, 34, 44, 46, 58